JN305578

Spiritual Messages given in English

SPIRITUAL MESSAGES FROM THE GUARDIAN SPIRIT OF
PRESIDENT
ASSAD

アサド大統領の
スピリチュアル・メッセージ

Ryuho Okawa
大川隆法

本霊言は、2013年9月11日(写真上・下)、幸福の科学総合本部にて、
質問者との対話形式で公開収録された。

アサド大統領の
スピリチュアル・メッセージ

Spiritual Messages from
the Guardian Spirit of President Assad

Preface

Any god who cannot understand "Love" is not real. "Punishment" is not the main task of God. Without love, everything is in vain. Without mercy, all the people of the world have abandoned their religions.

This *Spiritual Messages from the Guardian Spirit of President Assad* indicates that he is standing by Satan.

The next step of the world powers and the UN is to be cleared. Protect innocent people! This is my "Judgement."

September 17, 2013
Master of Happy Science
Ryuho Okawa

まえがき

　いかなる神であれ、「愛」を理解しないものは真実のものではない。「罰」は神の主たる任務には非ず。
　愛なくしては、すべては空しい。慈悲がなかったら、世界の諸民族は宗教を捨て去っていただろう。
　このアサド大統領守護霊の霊言は、彼がサタンとともにあることを示している。
　世界の大国や国連の次なるステップは明確である。罪なき人々を護るのだ！　これが私の「判断」である。

2013年9月17日
幸福の科学グループ創始者兼総裁
大川隆法

Contents

Preface 2

1 Summoning the Guardian Spirit of Assad in the Name of Elohim, the God of the Middle East 14

2 The Guardian Spirit of Assad Admits, "Of Course!" in Regard to Chemical Weapon Use 28

3 The Guardian Spirit of Assad Says, "Bad People Are Those Who Act Against My Will, My Will is the Same as God" 38

4 He Claims, "Countries Which Have Atomic Bombs Can Say Nothing About Chemical Weapons" 50

5 "I Do Not Feel Guilty About Killing More than 100,000 of My People" 58

6 On the Word "Terrorist" and the Legitimacy of the Shia Sect 66

7 "We Already Have Several Hundred Missiles" 76

8 "Democracy is Not Efficient in Arabic Countries" 90

目　次

まえがき　　3

1　中東の神エローヒムの名において
　　アサド守護霊を招霊する　　15
2　化学兵器の使用を「当然だ」と認める
　　アサド守護霊　　29
3　「悪人とは私に背く者。私の意志は神と同じ」
　　と言うアサド守護霊　　39
4　「原爆を持っている国は化学兵器について何も
　　言えない」と主張　　51
5　自国民を10万人以上殺したことに
　　「罪悪感はない」　　59
6　「テロリスト」という言葉と、
　　シーア派の正統性について　　67
7　「ミサイルはすでに何百基もある」　　77
8　「アラブ諸国では、民主主義は
　　効果的ではない」　　91

9 Don't the People Need Liberty or Happiness?	102
10 The Guardian Spirit of Assad Claims, "I'm a Part of Allah"	114
11 The Nobel Peace Prize Winner President Obama is a Bad Guy	118
12 The Guardian Spirit of Assad Insists, "Syria Used to Be the 'Spiritual Center of the World,' Human Rights Are Something Unbelievable"	132
13 Japan Should Fight Against America Again and Kill Obama	144
14 Justice is to Kill Those Who Disobey the Orders of God	160
15 The Guardian Spirit of Assad Persistently Denies Killing His Own People	172
16 In His Past Life, He Was a Relative of Ramses of Egypt	184
17 "Push Prime Minister Abe to Persuade the United States"	192
18 After Interviewing the Guardian Spirit of President Assad	202

9	自由も幸福も、国民には必要ないのか	103
10	「私はアッラーの一部」と主張する アサド守護霊	115
11	ノーベル平和賞受賞のオバマ大統領は 「悪いやつ」	119
12	シリアはかつての「世界の霊的中心」、人権は 「信じ難いもの」と主張するアサド守護霊	133
13	日本に望むことは「アメリカともう一度戦って オバマを殺せ」	145
14	正義とは「神の命令に背く者を殺すこと」	161
15	「私は自国民を殺していない」と執拗(しつよう)に否定 するアサド守護霊	173
16	過去世は「エジプトのラムセスの 一族だった」	185
17	「アメリカを説得するよう安倍首相に 圧力を」	193
18	アサド大統領の守護霊インタビューを 終えて	203

This book is the transcript of spiritual messages given by the guardian spirit of Syrian President Assad.

These spiritual messages were channeled through Ryuho Okawa. However, please note that because of his high level of enlightenment, his way of receiving spiritual messages is fundamentally different from other psychic mediums who undergo trances and are completely taken over by the spirits they are channeling.

Each human soul is made up of six soul siblings, one of whom acts as the guardian spirit of the person living on earth. People living on earth are connected to their guardian spirits at the innermost subconscious level. They are a part of people's very souls, and therefore, exact reflections of their thoughts and philosophies.

It should be noted that these spiritual messages are opinions of the individual spirits and may contradict the ideas or teachings of the Happy Science Group.

The spiritual messages and questions were spoken in English, but the closing comments were spoken in Japanese. English translations have been provided for this part.

本書は、シリア大統領アサド氏の守護霊の霊言を収録したものである。

　「霊言現象」とは、あの世の霊存在の言葉を語り下ろす現象のことをいう。これは高度な悟りを開いた者に特有のものであり、「霊媒現象」（トランス状態になって意識を失い、霊が一方的にしゃべる現象）とは異なる。

　また、人間の魂は６人のグループからなり、あの世に残っている「魂の兄弟」の１人が守護霊を務めている。つまり、守護霊は、実は自分自身の魂の一部である。

　したがって、「守護霊の霊言」とは、いわば、本人の潜在意識にアクセスしたものであり、その内容は、その人が潜在意識で考えていること（本心）と考えてよい。

　ただ、「霊言」は、あくまでも霊人の意見であり、幸福の科学グループとしての見解と矛盾する内容を含む場合がある点、付記しておきたい。

　なお、今回、霊人や質問者の発言は英語にて行われた。本書は、それに日本語訳を付けたものである（ただし、終節のコメントは日本語で語られており、それに英訳を付けている）。

Spiritual Messages from the Guardian Spirit of President Assad

September 11, 2013 at Happy Science General Headquarters

Spiritual Messages from the Guardian Spirit of Bashar al-Assad

アサド大統領の
スピリチュアル・メッセージ

2013年9月11日　幸福の科学総合本部にて
バッシャール・アル・アサド守護霊の霊言

Bashar al-Assad (1965~)

President of Syria. Second son of Former President Hafez al-Assad. The Assad family belongs to the Alawite sect, a minor sect within the Shia sect. Born in Damascus, Syria, Assad graduated from the medical school of Damascus University and attended postgraduate studies in London, specializing in ophthalmology. In 1994, he was called back to Syria after his elder brother and then to-be-president, Lieutenant Colonel Bassel al-Assad, died in a car crash. In July 2000, he was elected as the succeeding president by referendum. In August 2013, the Assad administration was suspected of using chemical weapons in the ongoing Syrian civil war, in the outskirts of the capital city of Damascus. Assad was voted twelfth in "The World's Worst Dictators 2010" conducted by *Parade*.

Questioner ※ In order of questions asked

Kazuhiro Ichikawa
  Senior Managing Director and Chief Director
  International Headquarters

Masashi Ishikawa
  Deputy Chief Secretary, First Secretarial Division
  Religious Affairs Headquarters

Mariko Isis
  Vice Chairperson of International Headquarters

Soken Kobayashi
  Vice Chairperson of Public Relations and Risk Management

※ Position titles are at the time of recording

バッシャール・アル・アサド（1965〜）

シリア・アラブ共和国大統領。ハーフィル・アル・アサド前大統領の次男。アサド家は、シーア派のうちでも、少数派であるアラウィ派に属す。シリアの首都ダマスカスに生まれ、ダマスカス大学医学部卒業後、ロンドンで眼科医の専門教育を受けるが、1994年、大統領の後継とされていた長兄バシル少佐が交通事故で死亡したため、シリアに呼び戻される。2000年7月、父の死去により、国民投票を経て、後任の大統領に就任。2013年8月、内戦が続くシリアの首都ダマスカス近郊で、アサド政権によって化学兵器が使用された疑いが浮上。ワシントン・ポストが発行する週刊誌「パレード」の「世界最悪の独裁者ランキング（2010年）」では、12位に選ばれている。

質問者 ※質問順

市川和博（幸福の科学専務理事 兼 国際本部長）

石川雅士（幸福の科学宗務本部第一秘書局担当局長）

イシス真理子（幸福の科学副理事長 兼 国際本部担当）

小林早賢（幸福の科学広報・危機管理担当副理事長）

※役職は収録当時のもの

1 Summoning the Guardian Spirit of Assad in the Name of Elohim, the God of the Middle East

Ryuho Okawa Today's theme is very difficult. It might be beyond the concept of religion. No one can give a correct answer to this problem because this is a "Syria problem." But, behind this problem there are two great countries. One is, of course, the United States of America and the other is Russia.

So, I just want to research the inner thinking of Mr. Bashar al-Assad of Syria. But this is not so easy. There is a lot of international diplomacy regarding this matter. How can we find the reality or justice? Where is God standing? Is God standing by the Assad regime or anti-Assad regime? Is God standing on the side of the United States or Russia? Is it essential for the world that the United States of America should continue to be the world's policeman or not?

Just a few minutes ago, I received a report about

1　中東の神エローヒムの名においてアサド守護霊を招霊する

大川隆法　本日のテーマは、非常に難しいテーマです。宗教の概念を超えているかもしれません。これは「シリア問題」ですから、この問題に正確な答えを出せる人はいないでしょう。ただ、その背後には、二つの大国があります。一つは、もちろん、アメリカ合衆国で、もう一つは、ロシアです。

　そこで、シリアのバッシャール・アル・アサド氏の内なる考えを調査してみたいと思います。ただ、これはそう簡単なことではありません。この件については、さまざまな国際外交が絡んでいます。私たちは、いかにして真実や正義を見出すことができるのか。神はどちらの側にいるのか、アサド政権か、反アサド政権か、合衆国側か、ロシア側か。「アメリカ合衆国が世界の警察官であり続けるべきかどうか」ということは、世界にとって重要なことなのか。

　ほんの数分前、私は、合衆国についての報告を受けま

the United States. It was President Obama's address. Today is the memorial day of September 11th. It's not a good memorial day, of course, but 12 years ago, the American people suffered a lot because of the attack of the terrorists. And on the same day, President Obama made a speech just one hour or two hours ago. What he said in this speech is very difficult to explain in short and in oral English because it is written in a formal way. Even if I read this (manuscript) directly you cannot understand the meaning of this context, so I will translate this. I read this just now because I just received this upstairs in this building (Happy Science General Headquarters). But before that, I read the Japanese translation of President Obama's address to the nation regarding Syria.

In that speech, Mr. President declared, "On August 21st, Assad used chemical weapons. This fact cannot be denied. This is one problem. The issue is how America and the international society should deal with this problem. If the United States of America

1　中東の神エローヒムの名においてアサド守護霊を招霊する

した。それは、オバマ大統領の演説についてです。今日は9月11日の記念日だからです。もちろん、良い記念日ではありませんが、12年前、アメリカ人は、テロリストの攻撃によって大変苦しみました。そして、オバマ大統領は、同じ日の、ほんの1〜2時間前に演説を行ったのです。その中で彼が言ったことを、手短に、しかも話し言葉でお伝えするのは、非常に困難です。彼の英語は、格式ばった形で書かれているからです。私がこれ(演説原稿)をそのまま読み上げても、みなさんには意味が分からないでしょうから読みませんが、こちらを翻訳したいと思います。何しろ、私はそれを、このビル(幸福の科学総合本部)の上の階で渡されて、まだ見たばかりなのです。ただ、その前に、オバマ大統領の、シリアに関する演説の日本語翻訳版は読みました。

　その演説によると、合衆国大統領は、「この8月21日に、アサドが化学兵器を使った。この事実は否定できない。これが一つ。問題は、アメリカや国際社会が、この問題にどう対処すべきか、ということである。もし、アメリカ合衆国が何の行動もとらなければ、アサド政権は、こ

doesn't do anything, the Assad administration will continue to use chemical weapons."

But now, President Obama is just thinking about using a targeted military attack only. Whether this will be enough or not, no one can say at this time. But, President Obama said he can show by this fact, this targeted military attack, that using chemical weapons is not allowed in the international society. President Obama can promise that, but it does not lead to the conclusion that a targeted attack can destroy Assad's military authority. So, no one can tell at this point, the situation that will follow this attack and about the future society because the American and French cruisers are already there. A Russian cruiser is also there because Russia has a military base on the seaside of Syria.

So, it can change into a trigger of a world war. For example, if Assad attacks Israel, at the time, Israel will also, of course, attack Syria. And it will lead to another conflict of the Arabian countries, of course.

1　中東の神エローヒムの名においてアサド守護霊を招霊する

れからも化学兵器を使い続けるだろう」と宣言しました。

　ただ、現在、オバマ大統領は、限定的な軍事攻撃のみを考えています。それが十分か否かについては、現時点では、誰も何も言えません。しかし、オバマ大統領は、「この事実、つまり限定的な軍事攻撃によって、『化学兵器の使用は、国際社会では許されないのだ』と示すことができる」と言っています。オバマ大統領は、そのことについては約束できますが、ただ、それがすなわち、「限定的攻撃によってアサド軍事政権を転覆させることができる」という結論に至るわけではありません。したがって、この攻撃のあと、どういう状況になるか、どのような未来社会になるのかについては、現時点では誰にも分かりません。アメリカの巡洋艦やフランスの巡洋艦がすでに（地中海に）いるからです。ロシアはシリアの沿岸部に軍事基地を持っているので、ロシアの巡洋艦もすでにいます。

　ですから、これは、世界戦争の引き金になる恐れがあります。たとえば、もし、アサド氏がイスラエルを攻撃すれば、イスラエルも当然、シリアを攻撃するでしょう。それは、当然ながら、アラブ諸国における新たな紛争を

Half of the Arabian countries agree with Assad, but the other half of the Arabian countries disagree with him. There are the military states of Russia and China on one side and on the other side is the United States, France and the U.K. The U.K. is, at this point, not so assertive to attack the Assad regime, but this might be similar to the situation during the Cold War.

The other point is that this war or, perhaps it is not a war and just a conflict, or it may stop short of a conflict, I cannot say exactly, but this Syria problem will be the test of the next stage of the Iranian problem, the Iran and Israel problem. There is also the China problem and the North Korean problem.

Then I want to say the following: In the last paragraph of his brief speech, President Obama said, "America is not the world's policeman. Terrible things happen across the globe, and it is beyond our means to right every wrong." It means that he himself thinks that his targeted military attack might fail and America cannot be the world's policeman anymore.

1　中東の神エローヒムの名においてアサド守護霊を招霊する

もたらすことになるでしょう。アラブ諸国の半数はアサド氏に賛成していますが、残りの半数は反対しています。そして、一方には、軍事国家であるロシアと中国があり、もう一方には合衆国・フランス・イギリスがあります。イギリスは、現時点では、アサド政権を攻撃することにあまり積極的ではありませんが、「これは、かつての冷戦のような状況である」と言えるかもしれません。

　この戦争は、あるいは戦争ではなく、単なる紛争かもしれないし、紛争になる前に終わるかもしれないので、正確なことは言えませんが、ただ、もう一つの論点としては、「このシリア問題が、イラン問題、イラン対イスラエル問題の、次なるステージのテストになる」ということです。さらには、中国問題と北朝鮮問題もあります。

　そこで、私が言いたいのは、こういうことです。オバマ大統領は、この短い演説の最後のパラグラフ（段落）で、「アメリカは『世界の警察官』ではない。地球の至るところで悲惨なことが起こるが、すべての悪を正すのは、我々の財政力を超えている」と言いました。つまり、彼自身、「限定的軍事攻撃は失敗するかもしれず、もはやアメリカは『世界の警察官』ではいられなくなる」と考えている

In this context, we can read it in this way. It sounds very strange and if this is the correct meaning of Mr. Obama, it is the final decision that America is no more a superpower of the world. I think that the American president admitted and agreed to this fact. So, it will, of course, influence the Japanese and Chinese problem or North Korean problem.

Anyway, it is very difficult but we will do our best. We must go beyond the limits of a religion and go as far as we can. We must be the top journalists of the world. No one can interview President Assad in this difficult situation and find out his real point, his consciousness; I mean his hidden consciousness, "under" consciousness and inner consciousness. So, it will be the first experience for President Assad. I will use the super power of remote viewing and the power which can read the mind of another person who is living on the other side of the Earth. These are special psychic powers. I will use both these powers. If possible, we must reach a conclusion on

1　中東の神エローヒムの名においてアサド守護霊を招霊する

わけです。この文脈では、そのように読めます。これは非常に奇妙に聞こえます。もし、これがオバマ氏の真なる意図であるなら、「アメリカは、もはや世界の超大国ではない」という最終決断になります。アメリカの大統領が、この事実に同意し、認めたことになると思います。ですから、これは当然、日本と中国の問題、また北朝鮮問題にも影響します。

　いずれにしても、非常に難しいことですが、最善を尽くすつもりです。宗教の限界を超えて、行けるところまで行かなければなりません。私たちは、世界のトップジャーナリストでなければなりません。この難しい状況の中で、アサド大統領にインタビューして、彼の本心、つまり隠された意識、潜在意識、内面意識を探り出すことができる人はいません。これは、アサド大統領にとっては、初めての体験です。私は、遠隔透視のスーパーパワーと、地球の反対側に住む人の心でも読み取ることのできる力を使います。これは、特別な霊能力です。これらの力を両方使います。可能であれば、アサド大統領が正しい心を持っているのかどうか、彼が悪人であるか否か、あるいは、体制側による攻撃が正しいのか、それとも反

whether President Assad has the Right Mind or not, whether he's evil or not and whether the attacking of the regime side is correct or the anti-regime side is correct.

President Obama said that the fact of whether he used chemical weapons or not is the criterion of good or evil, but it is not enough. We are a religious group, so we must think about which side is right from the eyes of God. Or, if plural gods are there and their criteria of righteousness are conflicting now, I must make another decision from the upper side. So, it's not so easy. But I will try.

Please ask good questions and check the reality of the spiritual phenomenon. And please go into the depths of Bashar al-Assad. Since I am just starting, I don't know exactly whether we will go deep into the darkness or deep into the light world, I don't know exactly. I will start now. OK?

Then I'll call Mr. Bashar al-Assad, the president of Syria. I will call Assad's guardian spirit, not another

1　中東の神エローヒムの名においてアサド守護霊を招霊する

体制側が正しいのか、結論を導き出したいと思います。

　オバマ大統領は、「『化学兵器を使ったかどうか』という事実が善悪の基準だ」と言いましたが、それでは十分ではありません。私たちは宗教団体ですから、神の目から見て、どちらが正しいのかを考えなければなりません。あるいは、もし、複数の神がいて、彼らの正しさの基準が現在対立しているのであれば、私は、より高い次元から、別の判断を下さなければなりません。ですから、簡単なことではありません。しかし、やってみます。

　どうか、いい質問をして、霊現象の真実を確かめてください。そして、バッシャール・アル・アサド氏の深い部分まで入ってください。今から始めるところですので、それが深い闇の中なのか、光の世界の中なのかは、よく分かりません。では、始めます。よろしいでしょうか。

　それでは、バッシャール・アル・アサド氏、シリアの大統領を呼びたいと思います。お呼びするのはアサド氏

person. It's the inner self of President Assad, so please don't misunderstand it to be a different person. It's the inner self of President Assad. OK?

OK, then, I'll summon the spirit. In the name of Elohim, I'll summon the guardian spirit of President Assad of Syria. I'll summon the inner self of President Assad. I'm going into the inner world of President Assad. Come over here. Please come across the great ocean and come down to Japan. This is Tokyo, Happy Science General Headquarters. I am Ryuho Okawa. In another name, I was called God Elohim, God Elohim. It is your God of the Middle East. I summon President Assad's inner consciousness. Come over here.

(about 13 seconds of silence)

1　中東の神エローヒムの名においてアサド守護霊を招霊する

の守護霊で、他の人ではありません。アサド大統領の「内なる自己」です。他の人と誤解しないでください。アサド大統領の「内なる自己」です。よろしいでしょうか。

　はい、それでは招霊します。エローヒムの名において、シリアのアサド大統領の守護霊を招霊します。アサド大統領の内なる自己を招霊します。これより、アサド大統領の内なる世界に参入します。こちらにお越しください。大海を渡って、日本に降りてきてください。ここは、東京の、幸福の科学の総合本部です。私は大川隆法です。またの名を、エローヒム神と呼ばれていました。エローヒム神です。中東のあなたがたの神です。アサド大統領の内なる意識を招霊します。こちらにお越しください。

（約13秒間の沈黙）

2 The Guardian Spirit of Assad Admits, "Of Course!" in Regard to Chemical Weapon Use

Ichikawa President Assad? President Assad?

Assad's Guardian Spirit★ Ahh, uhh, ahh, mmm.

Ichikawa Do you understand my English?

Assad's G.S. Ah. Just a moment. Just a moment. Just, just a moment.

Ichikawa Yes.

Assad's G.S. Huh? What kind of trial is this?

Ichikawa This is Happy Science General Headquarters.

★Assad's Guardian Spirit will be noted as Assad's G.S. from this point on.

2　化学兵器の使用を「当然だ」と認める アサド守護霊

市川　アサド大統領でしょうか。アサド大統領でしょうか。

アサド守護霊　ああ、うう、ああ、うーん。

市川　私の英語が分かりますでしょうか。

アサド守護霊　ああ、ちょっと待って。ちょっと待って、ちょっと。ちょっと待って。

市川　分かりました。

アサド守護霊　ん？　これは何の裁判だ？

市川　ここは、幸福の科学の総合本部です。

Assad's G.S. Happy Science General Headquarters? What is Happy Science?

Ichikawa It is a religious movement. It is a movement that goes beyond just a religion and creates happiness all over the world.

Assad's G.S. Japan?

Ichikawa Yes, this is Japan. Yes.

Assad's G.S. Happy Science?

Ichikawa Yes.

Assad's G.S. A religious group?

Ichikawa Yes.

Assad's G.S. Hmm... what's the connection

2　化学兵器の使用を「当然だ」と認めるアサド守護霊

アサド守護霊　幸福の科学の総合本部？　「幸福の科学」とは何だ？

市川　宗教運動です。単なる宗教を超えて、世界中に幸福を創る運動です。

アサド守護霊　日本？

市川　ええ、ここは日本です。ええ。

アサド守護霊　幸福の科学？

市川　そうです。

アサド守護霊　宗教団体？

市川　そうです。

アサド守護霊　うーん、君たちと私と、どんな関係があ

between us?

Ichikawa We are very concerned about the problems in Syria. Even though we are a religious organization, Master Okawa is giving a lot of advice about international politics and to the international society. So today…

Assad's G.S. I'm very, very, very, busy now. Mmm… I'm getting success.

Ichikawa Uh huh. Success?

Assad's G.S. Russia has very great power! And President Putin will succeed in protecting us.

Ichikawa Oh, I see. So you mentioned "success." What do you mean by "success"? Could you explain it in detail?

2 化学兵器の使用を「当然だ」と認めるアサド守護霊

るのかね？

市川　私たちは、シリア問題を非常に憂慮しております。私たちは宗教団体ではありますが、大川総裁は国際政治や国際社会にさまざまな助言をなされています。ですから本日は……。

アサド守護霊　私は、今、すごくすごく、すごく忙しいんだよ。うん、もうすぐ成功するからね。

市川　そうですか。成功ですか？

アサド守護霊　ロシアは、非常に力があるからね！　だからプーチン大統領が、うまく我々を守ってくれるんだ。

市川　そうですか。「成功」とおっしゃいましたが、それはどういう意味でしょうか。詳しくご説明いただけますでしょうか。

Assad's G.S. Success means that President Obama will be able to do nothing against us. Hahahahahahahaha! Ahahahahaha! (does a fist pump) Win! Win! Win! (takes a victory pose) Ohh! Win!

Ishikawa However, Russia proposed that you surrender your chemical weapons. Yes. To international control. So, are you going to surrender them? Is it true?

Assad's G.S. Oh, no, no, no.

Ishikawa No?

Assad's G.S. Just hide! Hide the chemical weapons. It's easy. We just need one or two days. It's easy.

Ishikawa Yeah, so you will surrender just one part, right?

2　化学兵器の使用を「当然だ」と認めるアサド守護霊

アサド守護霊　成功とは、「オバマ大統領は、我々に対して、何もできない」ということだよ。ハハハハハハハハ。アーッハッハッハッハッハ。（ガッツポーズ）勝つぞ、勝つぞ、勝つぞ。（両手を上げて）ウォー！　勝つぞ！

石川　しかし、ロシアの提案は、あなたが化学兵器を手放すということですよ。ええ。国際管理にゆだねるということです。手放すつもりですか。本当ですか。

アサド守護霊　いやいや、まさか。しないよ。

石川　しない？

アサド守護霊　隠すだけさ！　化学兵器を隠すのさ。簡単だよ。１日か２日もあればできる。簡単なもんさ。

石川　そうですか。では、一部だけを手放すということですね？

Assad's G.S. After that we can make them again easily.

Ichikawa I want to confirm: Do you have chemical weapons?

Assad's G.S. Of course!

Ichikawa Of course…

Assad's G.S. A lot of chemical weapons! A lot! We are a great power in the Middle East (laughs)!

Ichikawa Did you use chemical weapons?

Assad's G.S. Of course. Of course! I'm a great president.

2　化学兵器の使用を「当然だ」と認めるアサド守護霊

アサド守護霊　そのあと、また簡単に作れるからね。

市川　確認したいのですが、化学兵器を持っているのですか？

アサド守護霊　当たり前だろう！

市川　当たり前……。

アサド守護霊　大量の化学兵器をな！　大量だよ！　我々は中東の大国である（笑）！

市川　化学兵器を使ったのでしょうか？

アサド守護霊　当然だよ。当然！　私は偉大(いだい)な大統領だからね。

3 The Guardian Spirit of Assad Says, "Bad People Are Those Who Act Against My Will, My Will is the Same as God"

Assad's G.S.   Bad people must perish from this earth!

Isis   What do you mean by bad people?

Assad's G.S.   Bad people are the people who act against my will!

Isis   Your will? Could you tell us about your will?

Assad's G.S.   Will?

Isis   Yes.

3 「悪人とは私に背く者。私の意志は神と同じ」と言うアサド守護霊

アサド守護霊　悪人は、この地上から滅ぼさなければならん！

イシス　「悪人」とは、どういう意味でしょうか。

アサド守護霊　悪人とは、私の意志に背く者だ！

イシス　あなたの意志ですか？　あなたの意志とは何ですか？

アサド守護霊　意志？

イシス　ええ。

3 The Guardian Spirit of Assad Says, "Bad People Are Those Who Act Against My Will, My Will is the Same as God"

Assad's G.S. My will is the same as God. God's Will! Because I'm a president. Hmph!

Ichikawa Which God?

Assad's G.S. The president is almighty!

Ichikawa Which God do you believe in?

Assad's G.S. Huh? God is God!

Ishikawa So you belong to the Alawites? The Alawite sect of Islam? Right? It's a very minor group.

Assad's G.S. Your pronunciation is very different. You must learn it again! You must go to London and use proper pronunciation.

Ishikawa You studied English in the U.K. So that's

3 「悪人とは私に背く者。私の意志は神と同じ」と言うアサド守護霊

アサド守護霊 私の意志とは、神と同じさ。神の意志だよ！ 私は、大統領だからね。フン！

市川 どの神でしょうか？

アサド守護霊 大統領は、全能なんだ！

市川 あなたは、どの神を信じていらっしゃるのですか？

アサド守護霊 何？ 神は、神だよ！

石川 あなたは、アラウィ派に属していらっしゃいますよね？ イスラム教のアラウィ派に？ そうですよね？ 非常に少数派です。

アサド守護霊 お前は、発音がすごくおかしい。もう一度、学び直せ！ ロンドンに行って、正しい発音を使えるようになれ。

石川 あなたは、イギリスで英語を学ばれたんですよね。

why your pronunciation is British English.

Assad's G.S. You are using very "underdeveloped" English. New York uses a very low level English; it's barbaric.

Isis OK, may I ask a question?

Assad's G.S. OK, a lady. Oh.

Isis As you said, you have used chemical weapons...

Assad's G.S. Of course! Definitely! No problem!

Isis The United States once said that they are going to make a military intervention in the Syrian crisis soon. But, I think it will engulf Iran, Lebanon and Russia in a war and it might develop into World War III. How do you feel about this?

3 「悪人とは私に背く者。私の意志は神と同じ」と言うアサド守護霊

ですから、あなたの発音は、イギリス英語なんですね。

アサド守護霊　お前は、非常に程度の低い英語を使っている。ニューヨークでは、非常にレベルの低い英語が使われていて、未開だ。

イシス　では、質問してもよろしいでしょうか。

アサド守護霊　よろしい。女性か。おお。

イシス　あなたは、「化学兵器を使った」とおっしゃいましたが……。

アサド守護霊　当然だ！　その通り！　問題ない！

イシス　合衆国は、一度、「シリア危機に軍事介入する」と発表しました。しかし、私は思うのですが、それでは、イランやレバノン、ロシアを戦争に巻き込み、第三次世界大戦へと広がってしまうのではないでしょうか。それについては、どう感じていらっしゃいますか。

3 The Guardian Spirit of Assad Says, "Bad People Are Those Who Act Against My Will, My Will is the Same as God"

Assad's G.S. Just a moment, just a moment. You are going way too far. World War III? No, no, no. Mr. Obama said that they will abandon their role as the policeman of the world. That's the conclusion. It won't be a world war. There is no longer a world policeman.

Isis Yes, that's what he said, but at the same time, there is a possibility that America will decide to intervene in your country depending on the situation.

Assad's G.S. Why? Isn't that a bad thing? Don't you think so? That's a bad thing. It's like China attacking Japan. It's kind of like that. It's the same. Same thing!

Isis So, don't you think that using chemical weapons is a bad thing?

Assad's G.S. It's OK. I'm the president. I have the

3 「悪人とは私に背く者。私の意志は神と同じ」と言うアサド守護霊

アサド守護霊　ちょっと待って、ちょっと待ってくれ。あなたは飛躍しすぎだ。第三次世界大戦だって？　いや、いや、いや。オバマ氏は、「『世界の警察官』をやめる」と言ったんだ。それが結論だよ。世界大戦じゃない。もう、「世界の警察官」はいないんだ。

イシス　ええ、彼はそう言いましたが、同時に、状況によってはあなたの国に介入する可能性があります。

アサド守護霊　なぜだ？　それは悪いことではないか。違うか？　それは悪いことだ。中国が日本を攻撃するようなものだ。そのようなものだ。それと同じだ。同じことだ！

イシス　では、あなたは、「化学兵器を使うことは悪いことだ」とは思わないのでしょうか。

アサド守護霊　問題ないよ。私は大統領なんだから。私

right to use weapons.

Ichikawa But, it's against the international rules of the world.

Assad's G.S. Every weapon. All weapons. I'm a sovereign power of this country. I'm the president. I was elected by the people of this country.

Kobayashi Does the government of Russia acknowledge your use of chemical weapons? Really?

Assad's G.S. Ah, Russia…

Kobayashi Russia also supports you?

Assad's G.S. We're friends, friends, friends. Russia is a friend. Friends, of course, help each other, right? Russia has a military base in Syria. They must fight against every enemy.

には、武器を使う権利があるんだ。

市川　しかし、それは国際法に反しています。

アサド守護霊　あらゆる武器だ。すべての武器をだ。私がこの国に君臨しているんだ。私が大統領なんだ。私は、この国の人々に選ばれたんだ。

小林　ロシア政府は、あなたが化学兵器を使ったことを承知しているのでしょうか。本当でしょうか。

アサド守護霊　ああ、ロシア……。

小林　ロシアも、あなたを支持している？

アサド守護霊　友達だよ、友達、友達。ロシアは友達なんだ。友達は助け合うのが当然だろう？　ロシアは、シリアに軍事基地を持っている。彼らは、あらゆる敵と戦わねばならない。

3 The Guardian Spirit of Assad Says, "Bad People Are Those Who Act Against My Will, My Will is the Same as God"

Kobayashi But Putin declared that if Syria used chemical weapons, he will not support Syria. What's your comment on this?

Assad's G.S. No, no. That's not it. Don't rely on what the politician says. No, no. That isn't so.

Kobayashi The whole world is speaking ill of you.

Assad's G.S. Ah, OK. Please "delete" him (referring to Kobayashi.)

(audience laughs)

Assad's G.S. OK. (referring to Kobayashi) He is crazy, so please stop him.

3 「悪人とは私に背く者。私の意志は神と同じ」と言うアサド守護霊

小林　しかし、プーチンは、「もしシリアが化学兵器を使ったら、シリアを支持しない」と発言しました。それについてのコメントは？

アサド守護霊　いやいや、違う。そうじゃない。政治家の発言を信用してはいけない。違うんだ。

小林　世界中が、あなたのことを、悪く言っていますよ。

アサド守護霊　ああ、分かった。彼（小林）をどうにかしてくれ。

（会場笑）

アサド守護霊　分かった。彼（小林）は狂ってる。やめさせてくれ。

4 He Claims, "Countries Which Have Atomic Bombs Can Say Nothing About Chemical Weapons"

Ichikawa OK. I have a question about chemical weapons. Did you make the chemical weapons in your country?

Assad's G.S. Oh, it's easy.

Ichikawa Did you import from other countries?

Assad's G.S. Of course we imported them. But we can make them ourselves, too. We can make them. We have the power.

Ichikawa Which countries did you import from?

Assad's G.S. Ah, of course, China, North Korea and sometimes Iran and other countries. They all have

4 「原爆を持っている国は化学兵器について何も言えない」と主張

市川　分かりました。化学兵器について、一つ質問があります。化学兵器は、ご自身の国で作られたのでしょうか。

アサド守護霊　ああ、簡単だよ。

市川　他の国から輸入されたのでしょうか。

アサド守護霊　当然、輸入もした。でも、自分たちでも作れる。我々も作れる。我々には力がある。

市川　どちらの国から輸入されたのでしょうか。

アサド守護霊　そりゃあ、もちろん、中国、北朝鮮、それから、時々はイランや他の国々からもだ。彼らはみんな、

chemical weapons. America, Russia, China, U.K. and France all have chemical weapons, too.

Ichikawa But, they don't use chemical weapons. But you used them.

Assad's G.S. No, no, no. They use all kinds of weapons. Chemical weapons are just one of them. They have Atomic Bombs, too. Countries which have Atomic Bombs can say nothing about chemical weapons. These countries are bad. They are evil. They should be perished from earth. We only have chemical weapons. We only have Sarin.

Ichikawa You only have Sarin...

Assad's G.S. It is a small weapon!

Ichikawa So you don't have Atomic Bombs?

4 「原爆を持っている国は化学兵器について何も言えない」と主張

化学兵器を持っている。アメリカも、ロシアも、中国も、イギリスも、フランスも、みんな化学兵器を持っているよ。

市川　ただ、彼らは化学兵器を使いません。しかし、あなたは使いました。

アサド守護霊　いやいや、違う。彼らはあらゆる武器を使っている。化学兵器は、その一つに過ぎない。彼らは原爆(げんばく)も持っている。原爆を持っている国は、化学兵器については何も言えないはずだ。彼らは、悪だ。悪者だ。彼らこそ、地上から滅(ほろ)ぶべきだ。我々は、化学兵器を持っているだけだ。我々は、サリンしか持っていない。

市川　サリンしか持っていないと……。

アサド守護霊　小さな武器だよ！

市川　では、原爆は持っていないのですか。

Assad's G.S. Um… yes.

Ichikawa Yes? Do you mean you have them?

Assad's G.S. Iran wants to have Atomic Bombs, because they must protect themselves against the attacks from Israel. Israel is also aiming to attack us, so we need them.

Ichikawa I see.

Assad's G.S. Of course.

Ichikawa I see. So, you have Atomic Bombs in your country.

Assad's G.S. If possible.

Ichikawa If possible.

4 「原爆を持っている国は化学兵器について何も言えない」と主張

アサド守護霊　うーん、そうだね。

市川　持ってる？　持ってるということですか？

アサド守護霊　イランは、原爆を持ちたがっている。イスラエルの攻撃から身を守らなければならないからね。そして、イスラエルは、我々のことも攻撃しようとして狙(ねら)っている。だから、必要なのだ。

市川　そうですか。

アサド守護霊　当然だ。

市川　分かりました。「自国に原爆を持っている」ということですね。

アサド守護霊　可能ならね。

市川　可能なら。

Assad's G.S. If, if, "if," President Obama attacked our military bases with their cruise missiles, at that time, Russia might lend us the lethal weapon (laughs). At that time, Israel can do nothing (laughs)!

Ishikawa Yes, however, in the CBS interview…

Assad's G.S. Ah, in the CBS interview. Yes, yes, I know, I know, I know.

Ishikawa Yes. You said, "There has been no evidence that I used chemical weapons against my own people."

Assad's G.S. Of course, of course, of course. I am a politician so, of course.

Ishikawa Ah, so, it's not true?

4 「原爆を持っている国は化学兵器について何も言えない」と主張

アサド守護霊 もし、もし、「もし」ということだが、もしオバマ大統領が巡航ミサイルで我々の軍事基地を攻撃したら、そのときには、ロシアが殺人兵器を貸してくれるだろうよ（笑）。そうなったら、イスラエルは、何もできない！（笑）

石川 ええ、しかし、CBSのインタビューでは……。

アサド守護霊 ああ、CBSのインタビューね。はい、はい、分かってる、分かってる。分かってるよ。

石川 ええ、あなたは「自国民に対して化学兵器を使ったという証拠は、何もない」とおっしゃっていました。

アサド守護霊 もちろん、もちろん。当然だ。私は政治家だから、当然だ。

石川 ああ、では、それは真実ではないと？

Assad's G.S. It's true for America, but it's not true for Syria, right? I'm not American.

5 "I Do Not Feel Guilty About Killing More than 100,000 of My People"

Ishikawa Additionally, one million or two million of your own people were displaced to Lebanon and other countries.

Assad's G.S. One million or two million escaped from our country? They should be killed.

Ishikawa And it was estimated that 100,000 of your people were killed.

Assad's G.S. 100,000 people were killed?

Ishikawa Approximately.

アサド守護霊　それは、アメリカにとっては真実だが、シリアにとっては真実ではないということだろう？　私はアメリカ人じゃないからね。

5　自国民を10万人以上殺したことに「罪悪感はない」

石川　それに加えて、100万人か200万人もの国民が、レバノンや他国に追いやられましたね。

アサド守護霊　100万人か200万人が国から逃亡したのか？　彼らは殺されるべきだな。

石川　そして、「10万人の国民が殺された」と推定されています。

アサド守護霊　10万人が殺された？

石川　だいたいですが。

Assad's G.S. No, no. They were killed by the anti-government forces.

Ishikawa Do you feel guilty about that?

Assad's G.S. No.

Ishikawa No?

Assad's G.S. No. I'm correct. I'm right. I have righteousness.

Ishikawa But your party is the Ba'ath Party, right? And its concepts are...

Assad's G.S. No problem, no problem.

Ishikawa Unity, liberty and socialism. So you don't support the concept of liberty?

5 自国民を10万人以上殺したことに「罪悪感はない」

アサド守護霊　いやいや、反政府軍に殺されたんだ。

石川　あなたは、それに対して、罪悪感を感じていらっしゃいますか。

アサド守護霊　いや。

石川　感じてない？

アサド守護霊　感じてないね。私は正しいのだから。私は正しい。正しさは私にあるのだ。

石川　しかし、あなたの政党は、バース党ですよね？　その理念は……。

アサド守護霊　問題ないね。問題ないよ。

石川　「統一」「自由」「社会主義」です。あなたは、「自由」の概念を支持されないのですか。

5 "I Do Not Feel Guilty About Killing More than 100,000 of My People"

Assad's G.S. *My* liberty.

Ishikawa So it's *your* party.

Assad's G.S. *My* party. Yes, of course.

Ichikawa You once appreciated the movement of the Arab Spring but later, you changed your attitude.

Assad's G.S. The Arab Spring was bad. And it's still bad.

Ichikawa Which point is bad?

Assad's G.S. Authority is very essential in Arabic countries. That's because we don't need any more democratic movement. It only means instability.

Ichikawa But you studied in London.

5　自国民を10万人以上殺したことに「罪悪感はない」

アサド守護霊　"私の"自由だ。

石川　つまり、それは"あなた"の政党だと。

アサド守護霊　"私の"政党だ。ええ、当然だよ。

市川　あなたは以前、「アラブの春」の運動を評価されていたのに、その後、態度を変えました。

アサド守護霊　「アラブの春」は、だめだった。今でもだめだ。

市川　どの点がだめなのですか。

アサド守護霊　アラブ諸国では、権威というものが非常に重要なんだ。私たちには、これ以上、民主化運動は必要ないからね。それは「不安定」でしかない。

市川　しかし、あなたはロンドンで勉強されたので。

5 "I Do Not Feel Guilty About Killing More than 100,000 of My People"

Assad's G.S. I'm a doctor, I'm a doctor.

Ichikawa You are familiar with democracy. Why are you against democracy so much?

Assad's G.S. The U.K. is far away from here, so it's "good old days." Now I am the responsibility itself so I must have great responsibility. I must be the Iron Man of Syria. I must fight against great countries like the United States and other European countries, and the countries that declare themselves as democratic countries. But they are quite different from our history. We are just walking our way so they cannot intervene. We can choose and select our way and our future. It's our liberty, our own liberty. It's not "Liberty Island's★ liberty." It's our liberty. It's Syrian liberty. Hm!

What I'm afraid of is... please check the darkness of his mind, I mean President Obama. He just wants to become an old-fashioned American president like the

★The island in New York, U.S.A. where the Statue of Liberty is located.

5 自国民を10万人以上殺したことに「罪悪感はない」

アサド守護霊 私は、医者だよ、医者。

市川 民主主義のことはよくご存じですよね。なぜ、そんなに民主主義に反対なのでしょうか。

アサド守護霊 イギリスは、ここから遠いから、もう「古き良き時代」だね。私は今、「責任」そのものなんだ。だから、大きな責任を負わなければならない。私は、シリアの「アイアンマン」でなければならない。私は、大国である合衆国や欧州、そして、「民主主義」を名乗る国と戦わなければならない。しかし、彼らは、我々の歴史とはかなりかけ離れている。我々は、ただ、自分たちの道を歩んでいるだけなんだから、彼らが介入することはできない。我々は、自らの道を、自らの未来を選べるのだ。我々の自由だ。我々自身の自由であって、「リバティ島[注]の自由」などではないのだ。我々の自由だ。シリアの自由だ。フン！

　私が恐れているのは……、彼の、オバマ大統領の"心の闇"を点検してくれよ。彼は、ブッシュ父子のような時代遅れのアメリカ大統領になりたがっているだけだ。

[注] アメリカ・ニューヨーク州の、自由の女神がある島の名。

father and son Bush. Obama is such kind of a Satan. That's what he is. He just wants to make our country into a country like Iraq or a politically unstable country like Egypt. It's not good. I'm good itself. I'm right. I'm completely right.

6 On the Word "Terrorist" and the Legitimacy of the Shia Sect

Ishikawa I'm not sure if you are absolutely right or not, but some American people do not support military intervention.

Assad's G.S. Yes, yes. That's right.

Ishikawa The reason is that the rebels who are being killed by your military are terrorists. Of course, not all rebels are terrorists, but some terrorist organizations like Al Qaeda and Hezbollah are joining the rebels. Is this true?

そういう悪魔が彼の実体だ。彼はただ、我々の国を、イラクのような国や、エジプトのような政治的不安定の国にしたいだけなんだ。それは良くない。私は、善そのものだ。私は正しい。全面的に正しいのだ。

6 「テロリスト」という言葉と、シーア派の正統性について

石川　あなたが絶対的に正しいかどうかは分かりませんが、アメリカ人の中には、軍事介入を支持していない人々もいます。

アサド守護霊　ああ、そうだ。

石川　その理由は、あなたの軍隊によって殺されている反政府軍が、テロリストだからです。もちろん、すべての反政府軍がテロリストであるわけではありませんが、アルカイダやヒズボラなど、いくつかのテロ組織が反政府軍に加勢しています。それは、本当ですか。

Assad's G.S. Don't use the word "terrorists." It has a political meaning and is used in a political context. Great countries sometimes use the word "terrorists" to mean those who protest against their power, great power or military power, but sometimes "terrorists" is just the resistance. The difference between a resistance movement and terrorism is very difficult. It's not terrorists or terrorism. It's just a resistance movement. A resistance movement is sometimes right and in that case it's not terrorism. It's a sad story but we only have a small amount of military weapons and military power so a resistance movement is the only way for us to protest against great countries. So don't easily use such kind of words.

Ishikawa I see. Actually, the rebels formed the National Coalition for Syrian Revolutionary and Opposition Forces, and not only the Arab League but other Western countries approved this coalition as a legitimate government. By the way, Turkey and other

6 「テロリスト」という言葉と、シーア派の正統性について

アサド守護霊 「テロリスト」という言葉を使うな。それは、政治的な意味であって、政治的に使われるものだ。大国は、自分たちの力、大きな力、軍事力に対して抗議する人達のことを指して、「テロリスト」という言葉を使うことがあるが、「テロリスト」とは、単に、抵抗勢力であることもある。抵抗運動とテロリズムの違いは、非常に難しい。それは、テロリストやテロ行為ではなく、単なる抵抗運動なのだ。抵抗運動は時として正しいこともあり、それはテロ行為ではない。悲しむべきことだが、我々には、軍用兵器や軍事力が少ししかないため、時として、抵抗運動をすることが大国に抗議する唯一の手段なのだ。だから、安易にその手の言葉を使うな。

石川　分かりました。実際、彼らは、シリア革命反体制勢力国民連立（シリア国民連合）を形成しました。そして、アラブ連盟だけでなく、他の欧米諸国もこの国民連合を合法的政府として認めました。ところで、トルコや他のアラブ諸国は、反政府軍に武器を提供しています。それ

Arabic countries are providing weapons to the rebels. Will you be able to stop that?

Assad's G.S. OK, OK. You are Japanese so you are just followers of the United States. You do not make decisions on and you have no opinion on justice. But keeping the sovereignty of the country is justice itself. So I'm not a bad person. I just want to keep this country peaceful. I just want to make the opposing party and the opposing rebels surrender, so this is the right thing to do. Yes. Even the United States will do the same thing. I am like Lincoln of the United States of America. If Lincoln was reborn in Syria... (audience laughs) don't laugh! If I were Lincoln, I would say, "I will do it. I will use chemical weapons and unite this country."

Ishikawa I have another question. There is the Muslim Brotherhood, right? The Muslim Brotherhood has been the enemy for your party. For

を止められるのですか？

アサド守護霊 分かった、分かった。あなたがたは日本人だから、合衆国に従っているだけだ。あなたがたは、正義について、何の判断もしないし、何の考えも持っていない。だが、国の主権を守ることは、正義そのものだ。だから、私は悪人なんかじゃない。この国の平和を維持したいだけだ。私はただ、対立政党、対立する反乱者たちを降伏させたいだけだ。だから、これは正しいことなのだ。そう。合衆国だって、同じことをするだろう。私は、アメリカ合衆国で言えば「リンカン」なんだよ。もし、リンカンがシリアに生まれ変わったら……、（会場笑）笑うな！　私がリンカンなら、「私はやります。化学兵器を使って、この国を統一します」と言うだろう。

石川　もう一つ、質問があります。ムスリム同胞団がありますよね？　ムスリム同胞団は、あなたの政党にとっては、ずっと敵でした。たとえば、1982年には、あなた

example, in 1982, your father killed more than 10,000 people, maybe, in Hama.

Assad's G.S. Only 10,000 people? No.

Ishikawa What do you think of the Muslim Brotherhood? For example, in Egypt, the former president was ousted and after that the country went into chaos.

Assad's G.S. That is something that is quite difficult. Japanese people cannot understand in regard to these groups because they have their own religious concept. So it is very difficult for you to understand. But we must protect Syria and Iran because there are Shiites in these two countries. So the Shia sect is the only orthodox sect. The Shia sect is the only orthodox Muslim. So these two countries must be protected from other countries' attacks. The Shia sect is the legitimate sect from Muhammad. That is why

6 「テロリスト」という言葉と、シーア派の正統性について

の父親は、ハマーで、おそらく1万人以上の人々を殺しました。

アサド守護霊　たった1万人か？　違うだろう。

石川　ムスリム同胞団についてはどう思われますか。たとえば、エジプトでは、前大統領がその座を追われ、その後、国が混乱しました。

アサド守護霊　それは、非常に難しいんだ。日本人には、これらのグループについては理解できない。彼らには、独自の宗教的概念があるからだ。だから、あなたがたには、非常に理解し難いことだ。ただ、シリアとイランは守らなければならない。これら二つの国には、シーア派があるからだ。シーア派は、唯一の正統派だ。シーア派だけが、正統なイスラム教なのだ。だから、この二国は、他国の攻撃から守られなければならない。シーア派は、ムハンマドからの正統派なのだ。だから、我々は、自分の国を守らなければならない。

we must protect our country.

Ishikawa But your religious group is Alawite and maybe it's a minority group, right?

Assad's G.S. But it's a Shia sect.

Ichikawa But some say that, because you belong to a minority, Alawites, you are attacking people of the majority.

Assad's G.S. The majority is Satan-like people.

Ichikawa And you said you believe in God. So could you tell me…

Assad's G.S. Oh, I believe in God. God can only be seen through the Shia sect. The Sunni sect is quite different from Shia. Sunni is a man-made religion.

6 「テロリスト」という言葉と、シーア派の正統性について

石川　しかし、あなたはアラウィ派で、おそらく、少数派なのではないですか。

アサド守護霊　だが、シーア派だ。

市川　ただ、あなたが「アラウィ派という少数派に属しているからこそ、多数派の人々を攻撃しているのだ」という説もあるのですが。

アサド守護霊　多数派は、悪魔のようなやつらだよ。

市川　また、あなたは、「神を信じている」とおっしゃいました。そこで伺いたいのですが…。

アサド守護霊　ああ、神は信じているよ。神は、シーア派を通してのみ見ることができるのだ。スンニ派は、シーア派とはまったく違う。スンニ派は、人間が作った宗教だ。

Ishikawa Then the fundamental cause of civil war is religious conflict?

Assad's G.S. In some meaning, yes.

Ishikawa Or a huge income gap?

Assad's G.S. In some meaning, yes.

Ishikawa It's a little complicated.

Assad's G.S. Complicated? Yes, very complicated.

7 "We Already Have Several Hundred Missiles"

Ishikawa OK. I will change my question. President Obama and Senator John McCain said, "We will not send ground troops to Syria but we will conduct limited air strikes." So will that...

石川　では、内戦の根本的原因は、宗教的対立なのでしょうか。

アサド守護霊　ある意味では、そうだ。

石川　あるいは、大きな収入格差ですか。

アサド守護霊　ある意味では、そうだ。

石川　少し複雑ですね。

アサド守護霊　複雑？　そうだな。非常に複雑だ。

7　「ミサイルはすでに何百基もある」

石川　分かりました。質問を変えます。オバマ大統領やジョン・マケイン上院議員は、「シリアには、地上部隊は送らないが、限定的な空爆は行う」と言いました。それは……。

Assad's G.S. He is more of a bad person than me.

Ishikawa Is it effective without sending ground troops?

Assad's G.S. It will be effective in killing a lot of people. I cannot kill so many people but he can. He can kill 100,000 people by air strike. He is more of a bad person than me.

Ishikawa America and other Western countries do not want to repeat the mistake they made in Iraq. They do not want to repeat the Iraq experience.

Assad's G.S. It was a mistake. A mistake. Yes.

Ishikawa Not a mistake, but they couldn't find the WMDs or Weapons of Mass Destruction.

Assad's G.S. I dare say that President Obama was

アサド守護霊　彼は、私以上に悪人だ。

石川　地上部隊を送らなくて、効果がありますか。

アサド守護霊　多くの人々を殺すには効果的だろうね。私にはそんなに多くの人を殺せないが、彼には殺せる。彼は、空爆で10万人殺せる。私以上の悪人だ。

石川　アメリカや他の西洋諸国は、イラクにおける間違いを繰り返したくないと思っています。彼らは、イラクでの経験を繰り返したくないのです。

アサド守護霊　間違いだ、間違い。そうだ。

石川　間違いではありませんが、彼らは、大量破壊兵器を見つけられませんでした。

アサド守護霊　あえて言うが、オバマ大統領は、イスラ

born as a Muslim. He must be worshipping Allah so he must obey my opinion.

Ishikawa He is not a Muslim. He is a Christian.

Assad's G.S. No, he is a Muslim. He was a Muslim. He converted to Christianity.

Ishikawa He is no longer a Muslim.

Assad's G.S. He must be hanged according to the Muslim teachings. He is a converted man so he must be killed by Muslim law.

Ishikawa Sorry but you did not answer my question. Is a limited attack effective or not?

Assad's G.S. Oh, it's effective in killing 100,000

ム教徒として生まれたんだ。彼は、アッラーを信仰しているはずだ。だから、彼は私の意見に従わなければならない。

石川　彼はイスラム教徒ではありません。彼はキリスト教徒です。

アサド守護霊　いや、彼はイスラム教徒だ。イスラム教徒だった。キリスト教に改宗したんだ。

石川　もうイスラム教徒ではありません。

アサド守護霊　イスラム教の教えでは、彼は絞首刑にならなければならない。改宗者だから、イスラム法によって殺されなければならない。

石川　すみません、私の質問にはお答えいただいていません。限定的な攻撃は効果的ですか、どうですか。

アサド守護霊　10万人を殺すには効果的だよ。

people.

Ishikawa But without sending ground troops they cannot overthrow or oust you.

Assad's G.S. He can make an attack but he cannot change this regime. He cannot change this authority, the Assad authority. He is just playing. I mean it's a game, a war game. He wants to play a war game as the president of the United States. This is just a game, an air strike show. He just wants to export destructive military weapons to other countries. So, this is just a show and in this show, he wants to kill 100,000 Syrians.

Ishikawa I see. Last week, a CBS interviewer interviewed you.

Assad's G.S. Uh huh.

7 「ミサイルはすでに何百基もある」

石川　しかし、地上部隊を送らなければ、あなたを退陣させることはできないでしょう。

アサド守護霊　彼は、攻撃はできるが、この体制を変えることはできない。この権力、アサド一族の権力を変えることはできない。彼は遊んでるだけだよ。つまり、ゲームさ。戦争ゲーム。彼は、合衆国大統領として、戦争ゲームがしたいだけなんだ。単なるゲームに過ぎない、空爆ショーだ。自分たちの軍事破壊兵器を他の国々に輸出したいだけなんだ。だから、これはショーに過ぎなくて、ショーのなかでシリア人を10万人も殺そうとしているんだ。

石川　分かりました。先週、あなたは、CBSのインタビューに応じられました。

アサド守護霊　ああ。

7 "We Already Have Several Hundred Missiles"

Ishikawa And it is said that you expressed concern that U.S. strikes would tip the military balance against your regime. So, you are especially afraid of American strikes.

Assad's G.S. But Russia will be against their attack.

Ishikawa However, I do not think Russia will send ground troops or intervene.

Assad's G.S. America also cannot send military troops, I mean the military cannot occupy our country. It's difficult for them to send a lot of military soldiers to our country because they need one million soldiers to occupy our country. It's difficult for them.

Ishikawa Russia has the one and only naval base in the Mediterranean Sea, so they want to protect that

7 「ミサイルはすでに何百基もある」

石川　そして、あなたが「アメリカの攻撃によって軍事面でのバランスが崩れ、政府側が不利になるのではないかとの懸念を表明した」といわれています。ですから、あなたは、特に、アメリカからの攻撃を恐れているわけです。

アサド守護霊　だが、ロシアは、アメリカの攻撃に反対する立場をとるだろうね。

石川　といっても、「ロシアは、地上部隊を送らない」あるいは「介入しない」と私は思います。

アサド守護霊　アメリカも、軍隊を送ることはできない。つまり、軍隊が、我が国を占領することはできないよ。我が国を占領するためには100万人の兵士が必要だから、それだけ多くの兵士を我が国に送り込むことは難しい。アメリカには難しいのさ。

石川　ロシアは、地中海で唯一の海軍基地を持っていますので、その基地を守りたいでしょう。

base.

Assad's G.S. America just wants to use their cruise missiles, but if Russia can also use the cruise missiles, it's even.

Ichikawa Some news media report that Syria purchased 40 missiles from North Korea. Is this true?

Assad's G.S. We bought a lot of missiles already.

Ichikawa From many countries?

Assad's G.S. Not only North Korea but also, of course, Russia and China.

Ichikawa Uh huh, I see.

Assad's G.S. We already have several hundred missiles and they are being moved. They are being

7 「ミサイルはすでに何百基もある」

アサド守護霊　アメリカは、巡航ミサイルを使いたいだけだ。しかし、もし、ロシアも巡航ミサイルを使えるなら、互角だね。

市川　「シリアは北朝鮮からミサイル40基を購入した」と伝える報道もありますが、ほんとうでしょうか。

アサド守護霊　ミサイルなら、もうたくさん買ったよ。

市川　いろんな国からですか。

アサド守護霊　北朝鮮だけでなく、もちろんロシアや中国からも。

市川　なるほど。

アサド守護霊　ミサイルはすでに何百基もあって、移動中だ。今もいろんなところへ移動していて、まだ狙われ

moved now, to a lot of places, and are not targeted yet. America cannot attack these missiles because we have a lot of military bases in our country and we have several hundred missiles. They cannot attack all the bases at the same time and destroy all the missiles. It's very difficult. We can camouflage, so it's very difficult. We already moved the missiles and are moving them even now.

Ichikawa Then, I would like to double check. Did you purchase nuclear weapons from some countries? I'm talking about nuclear weapons.

Assad's G.S. Nuclear weapons? Not yet, not yet. Not yet. Not yet. It's true. Not yet.

Ishikawa Do you have the intention or plan to purchase them?

Assad's G.S. I have the intention but not yet.

7 「ミサイルはすでに何百基もある」

ていない。我が国には、基地がたくさんあり、数百基ものミサイルがあるので、アメリカはそれらのミサイルを攻撃することができない。同時に攻撃して、すべてのミサイルを破壊することなど、できはしない。それは困難を極めることだ。偽装することができるから、非常に難しい。すでにミサイルを移動させたし、今も移動させているよ。

市川　では、もう一度確認させてください。あなたは、複数の国から核兵器を購入されましたか。核兵器を、です。

アサド守護霊　核兵器？　まだまだだ。まだだ。まだだ。ほんとうに、まだだ。

石川　購入する意志、あるいは計画はありますか？

アサド守護霊　意志はあるが、まだだ。

Ichikawa Not yet.

8 "Democracy is Not Efficient in Arabic Countries"

Ishikawa When you were young, you were a very quiet and reserved person, and you were supposed to become a medical doctor.

Assad's G.S. Medical doctor, yes, yes, yes.

Ishikawa That is why you studied in the U.K.

Assad's G.S. I'm still a doctor. I want to perform a medical operation on this country. If there is a bad part in the body and we find that part, we just need to cut it out from the body. This is the job of a doctor.

Ishikawa I see. I think that maybe your wife worked in the U.K. as a banker. She is…

市川　まだなんですね。

8 「アラブ諸国では、民主主義は効果的ではない」

石川　あなたは、若い頃、とても静かで控えめな方で、医者になるはずでした。

アサド守護霊　医者、そう、そう、そう。

石川　そのために、イギリスに留学されました。

アサド守護霊　私は今でも医者だよ。この国に外科手術を施したいんだ。体に悪い部分があって、それを見つけたら、体から切除するまでだ。それが医者の仕事さ。

石川　なるほど。あなたの奥様は、確か、イギリスで銀行員として働かれていたと思います。彼女は……。

Assad's G.S. "A Rose in the Desert."

Ishikawa Yes, she is Sunni, right?

Assad's G.S. Sunni, yeah.

Ishikawa She was born and raised in the U.K. and has an affinity towards democracy and many people expected that you would change or transform...

Assad's G.S. I tried.

Ishikawa Syria?

Assad's G.S. I tried.

Ishikawa You tried?

Assad's G.S. Once.

料金受取人払郵便

赤坂支店
承　認

5196

差出有効期間
平成26年5月
5日まで
(切手不要)

| 1 | 0 | 7 | 8 | 7 | 9 | 0 |
112

東京都港区赤坂2丁目10−14
幸福の科学出版(株)
愛読者アンケート係 行

フリガナ お名前		男・女	歳
ご住所　〒　　　　　　　都道 　　　　　　　　　　　　府県			
お電話（　　　）　−			
e-mail アドレス			
ご職業	①会社員 ②会社役員 ③経営者 ④公務員 ⑤教員・研究者 ⑥自営業 ⑦主婦 ⑧学生 ⑨パート・アルバイト ⑩他（　　　）		

ご記入いただきました個人情報については、同意なく他の目的で
使用することはございません。ご協力ありがとうございました。

愛読者プレゼント☆アンケート

『アサド大統領のスピリチュアル・メッセージ』のご購読ありがとうございました。今後の参考とさせていただきますので、下記の質問にお答えください。抽選で幸福の科学出版の書籍・雑誌をプレゼント致します。(発表は発送をもってかえさせていただきます)

1 本書をお読みになったご感想
(なお、ご感想を匿名にて広告等に掲載させていただくことがございます)

2 本書をお求めの理由は何ですか。
①書名にひかれて　　②表紙デザインが気に入った　　③内容に興味を持った

3 本書をどのようにお知りになりましたか。
①新聞広告を見て [新聞名：　　　　　　　　　　　　　　　　　　　　　　　]
②書店で見て　　　③人に勧められて　　　④月刊「ザ・リバティ」
⑤月刊「アー・ユー・ハッピー?」　　⑥幸福の科学の小冊子
⑦ラジオ番組「天使のモーニングコール」「元気出せ! ニッポン」
⑧BSTV番組「未来ビジョン」　　⑨幸福の科学出版のホームページ
⑩その他 (　　　　　　　　　　　　　　　　　　　　　　　　　　　　　)

4 本書をどちらで購入されましたか。
①書店　　　②インターネット (サイト名　　　　　　　　　　　　　　　)
③その他 (　　　　　　　　　　　　　　　　　　　　　　　　　　　　　)

5 今後、弊社発行のメールマガジンをお送りしてもよろしいですか。
　　　　　はい (e-mailアドレス　　　　　　　　　　　　　) ・ いいえ

6 今後、読者モニターとして、お電話等でご意見をお伺いしてもよろしいですか。(謝礼として、図書カード等をお送り致します)
　　　　　　　　　　　　はい ・ いいえ

弊社より新刊情報、DMを送らせていただきます。新刊情報、DMを希望
されない方は右記にチェックをお願いします。　☐DMを希望しない

8 「アラブ諸国では、民主主義は効果的ではない」

アサド守護霊　「砂漠のバラ」ね。

石川　はい、スンニ派の方ですね。

アサド守護霊　スンニ派だな。

石川　彼女はイギリスで生まれ育ち、民主主義と親和性のある方ですので、あなたに「変革ないし改革を行ってくれるだろう」と期待する人が、たくさんいました。

アサド守護霊　やろうとしたよ。

石川　シリアの？

アサド守護霊　やろうとした。

石川　試みられたのですか。

アサド守護霊　かつてはね。

Ishikawa Maybe last year or two years ago, you made revisions to the constitution which included eliminating the superiority of the Ba'ath Party. Now Syria has a one-party dictatorship. But are you going to change that and allow other parties?

Assad's G.S. It depends on our religion. I mean, Islam is similar to a one-man governance. It's very similar. One God, Allah, and all the people. It's the same regime. One president and the people.

Ichikawa But, in the United States, there are Christians and they believe in the one and only God but they have a democracy.

Assad's G.S. Democracy is very complicated and needs time, money and procedures. It takes a long time to get good results through the operations of the government. Democracy is not a good skill, technology or science. It might be useful in some

8 「アラブ諸国では、民主主義は効果的ではない」

石川　確か、昨年か一昨年、あなたは憲法を改正され、そして、バース党の優位性等を廃止されました。現在、シリアは一党独裁になっています。けれども、あなたは変革を行なって、他の政党も認めたいということでしょうか。

アサド守護霊　それは、我々の宗教にかかっている。つまり、「イスラム教は、独裁的な統治によく似ている」ということなんだよ。非常に似ている。唯一の神アッラーとすべての人間。同じ体制だ。1人の大統領と国民だから。

市川　しかし、アメリカは、キリスト教国で、唯一神を信じていますが、民主主義国です。

アサド守護霊　民主主義は非常に複雑で、時間と金と手続きを要する。政治の手続きでいい結果を得ようとしたら、時間のかかることが多いわけだ。民主主義は、あまりいい技能でもなければ、技術でも科学でもない。それが役に立つ国もあるかもしれないが、我が国や他のアラ

countries, but in our country or other Arabic countries, I think that democracy is not so sufficient and efficient.

Ishikawa So, after the Arab Spring, for example, in Egypt, the Muslim Brotherhood or President Morsi…

Assad's G.S. Egypt is in very bad condition now, you know? So that was a bad thing. The Arab Spring is said to be a good thing but in reality, it brought about a lot of massacres, so the result was bad. The result was bad; the fruits were bad. Then, the Arab Spring was bad initially.

Ishikawa Ironically, I think many young people in Egypt, especially in the cities, wanted more and more liberty.

Assad's G.S. No, no, no, no, no.

ブ諸国では、民主主義は十分かつ効果的なものではないと思うなあ。

石川　「アラブの春」の後、たとえばエジプトでは、ムスリム同胞団、あるいはモルシ大統領は……。

アサド守護霊　エジプトの現在の状況は、すごく悪い。そうだろう？　だから、それは悪いことなんだ。「アラブの春」は、いいことのように言われているけれど、実際には大量殺戮(さつりく)を招いたんだから、結果は悪かった。結果、"果実"は悪かったんだ。ということは、「アラブの春」は最初から悪かったんだ。

石川　皮肉なことですが、エジプトの、特に都市部の若者の多くは、もっともっと自由を求めていたと思います。

アサド守護霊　違う、違う、違う、違う、違う。

Ishikawa But, you know…

Assad's G.S. No, no, no, no, no, no, no.

Ishikawa After that the Muslim Brotherhood took over the regime and as a result they lost liberty. It's very ironic. What do you think of it?

Assad's G.S. In the Arabian world, we are suited to such kind of politics. I mean that the "control-under-one-king" style is suitable for the Arabic world, historically, traditionally and in the eyes of God. Democracy is the denial of God. It's a bad, bad, complicated method.

Ishikawa So, of course, democracy is not omnipotent and suitable for all countries. But in your opinion, maybe a one-party rule or dictatorship…

Assad's G.S. I'm a king. King. King.

8 「アラブ諸国では、民主主義は効果的ではない」

石川　ところが、ご存じのように……。

アサド守護霊　違う、違う、違う、違う、違う、違う、違う。

石川　その後、ムスリム同胞団が政権をとり、その結果、自由を失いました。とても皮肉な結果です。これについては、どう思われますか。

アサド守護霊　アラブ世界には、そんな政治形態が合ってるんだ。つまり、歴史的にも、伝統的にも、神の目から見ても、1人の王様のもとに統治されるスタイルが、アラブ世界には合ってるんだよ。民主主義は、神の否定だ。悪くて複雑な制度だね。

石川　もちろん、民主主義は、全能ではありませんし、すべての国に合っているわけではありませんが、あなたの考えでは、たぶん、一党支配あるいは独裁は……。

アサド守護霊　私は王なんだ。王、王だ。

Ishikawa King?

Assad's G.S. King or president, president. Yeah.

Ishikawa And Russia. It's like they have a king also…

Assad's G.S. Yeah. King. King also.

Ishikawa So you have a similar mentality?

Assad's G.S. King. King is good. King is akin to God. Yeah.

Isis But I think that God wants to help people and love people.

Assad's G.S. No, no, no. God wants to punish people.

8 「アラブ諸国では、民主主義は効果的ではない」

石川　王？

アサド守護霊　王、あるいは大統領、大統領だ。そうだ。

石川　ロシアも、王政のような……。

アサド守護霊　そう、王政だ、同じく王政だ。

石川　あなたも同じような考え方をお持ちなのですね。

アサド守護霊　王だ。王はいい。王は神に近い。そうだ。

イシス　神は「人々を助けたい、愛したい」と望んでいると思います。

アサド守護霊　違う、違う、違う。神は、人を罰したいのだ。

Isis Really? Don't you want to make your people happier? Or like…

Assad's G.S. No, no, no, no. Punish bad people.

Isis Bad people?

Assad's G.S. That is the justice of God.

9 Don't the People Need Liberty or Happiness?

Isis You said that you have righteousness and that you are righteousness itself. But how do you feel about your people?

Assad's G.S. I, I, I, I am a medical doctor! A medical doctor's job is not to punish but to do surgery, to cut off the bad portion of the body.

イシス　本当ですか？　あなたは、「国民をもっと幸福にしたい」と思わないのですか。あるいは……。

アサド守護霊　いや、思わない。悪いやつらを罰するんだ。

イシス　悪い人たち、ですか。

アサド守護霊　それが、「神の正義」なんだ。

9　自由も幸福も、国民には必要ないのか

イシス　あなたは、「自分は正しい。自分が正しさそのものである」とおっしゃいましたが、国民については、どのように感じているのですか。

アサド守護霊　私、私、私、私は医者だ！　医者の仕事は、罰することではなく、外科手術、体の悪い部分を切除することだ。

9 Don't the People Need Liberty or Happiness?

Isis Yes, but…

Assad's G.S. It's the same (laughs)!

Isis But what about the good people in your country?

Assad's G.S. Good people? Good people are obedient to me. They are good people.

Isis In the past, a long time ago…

Assad's G.S. A long time ago.

Isis …in Arabic countries…

Assad's G.S. Arabic countries, uh huh.

Isis …dictatorship might have been good.

イシス　そうですが……。

アサド守護霊　同じだ（笑）！

イシス　では、あなたの国の善良な国民についてはいかがでしょうか。

アサド守護霊　善良な国民？　善良な国民は、私の言うことをきく。それが善良な国民だよ。

イシス　過去においては、遠い昔は……。

アサド守護霊　遠い昔。

イシス　アラブの国々では……。

アサド守護霊　アラブ諸国。はいはい。

イシス　独裁制もよかったかもしれません。

9 Don't the People Need Liberty or Happiness?

Assad's G.S. Uh huh.

Isis But in this world, people can connect to the Internet. Also, I think you yourself and many young people go abroad to study, right?

Assad's G.S. Ah…

Isis So, they know the liberty or the freedom that other people in other countries have.

Assad's G.S. People who went abroad, I mean, to Western countries brought to our country several diseases, some kind of illness of thinking, thought, bad thinking, virus-like thinking, so it's very bad indeed. You mentioned the Internet?

Isis Yes.

Assad's G.S. We should ban the Internet.

9　自由も幸福も、国民には必要ないのか

アサド守護霊　ああ。

イシス　でも、現代では、みんなインターネットを使うことができます。また、あなたご自身や、多くの若い人たちも、海外留学していると思います。そうですよね？

アサド守護霊　ああ。

イシス　ですから、彼らは、他の国の人たちが得ている自由を知っているのです。

アサド守護霊　海外に、要するに西欧諸国(せいおうしょこく)に行ったやつらは我が国に、病気、ある種の思想の病気、間違った考え、ウィルスのような考えを持ち込んだんだ。実に悪いことだ。お前は、「インターネット」と言ったな。

イシス　はい。

アサド守護霊　そのインターネットを禁止しないといか

Isis Yes, I know. You have restricted the freedom to use the Internet.

Assad's G.S. Yeah, it's true. Yeah, it's the right thing to do. Right. God's right! Yeah!

Isis God's right?

Assad's G.S. Yeah, the authority must judge the information – which is right and which is wrong – by doing so, people cannot inform each other of bad news or create news easily or freely. It's not good.

Isis But I think the people's happiness…

Assad's G.S. Happiness?

ん。

イシス　はい、分かっています。あなたはインターネットを使う自由を制限しましたから。

アサド守護霊　そう、その通り、それが正しいことなんだ。権利。神の権利だ！　そうだ！

イシス　神の権利？

アサド守護霊：そうだ、権威ある者が、どれが正しくてどれが間違っているか、情報を判定しなければならない。そうすれば、みんなが互いに間違ったニュースを伝え合ったり、簡単に自由にニュースをつくり出すことはできない。それはよくないことだからな。

イシス　ですが、私が思うのは、国民の幸福が……。

アサド守護霊　幸福？

Isis Uh huh.

Assad's G.S. No! They don't need happiness.

Isis No? They don't need happiness?

Assad's G.S. They don't need happiness (laughs)! Happiness is a… It belongs to God and it belongs to the king. Happiness is a king's belonging (laughs). They just need their wants, such as food or money, fulfilled. If the government supplies them with things essential for living, not amenities, it's enough.

Isis But…

Kobayashi That's a slave country! You have made a country where all people are just slaves.

Assad's G.S. It's good. It's Egyptian history. Egypt is a slave country (laughs).

9　自由も幸福も、国民には必要ないのか

イシス　はい。

アサド守護霊　いや！　彼らには幸福なんか必要ない。

イシス　必要ない？　彼らには幸福は必要ないのですか。

アサド守護霊　彼らには、幸福は必要ない！（笑）幸福は、神のものであり、王のものだ。幸福は王の所有物だ（笑）。国民は、必要が満たせれば、要は食べ物や金に困らなければ、それでいい。快適さというところまで行く前の、生活必需品が政府から支給されれば、それで十分なんだよ。

イシス　でも……。

小林　それでは、奴隷制の国家です！　あなたは、全員が奴隷の国家を作ったんです。

アサド守護霊　それはいいことだ。それはエジプトの歴史だよ。エジプトは、奴隷制の国家だよ（笑）。

Isis But the God that you believe in wants people to be happy, right?

Assad's G.S. It's a weak god. Weaker god. Weakest god. He cannot be a king.

Kobayashi God is mercy.

Assad's G.S. Mercy?

Kobayashi Yes!

Assad's G.S. Mercy is a political word.

Kobayashi No, mercy has a religious meaning!

9　自由も幸福も、国民には必要ないのか

イシス　でも、あなたが信じる神は、みんなに幸福になってもらいたいと願っているわけですよね。

アサド守護霊　そんなのは弱い神だ。弱いほうの神だ。一番弱い神だ。そんな神では、王になれないな。

小林　神は「慈悲(じひ)」です。

アサド守護霊　慈悲？

小林　そうです！

アサド守護霊　「慈悲」というのは、政治的な言葉だよ。

小林　違います。慈悲には宗教的な意味があるのです！

10 The Guardian Spirit of Assad Claims, "I'm a Part of Allah"

Ichikawa So, could you tell us the name of the God you believe in? You said, "God, God, God," but you didn't say God's name.

Assad's G.S. Ahh, God's name is hidden. Yes, God's name has been hidden historically. God's name now appeared as Bashar al-Assad. It's another name for God.

Ichikawa Are you referring to Allah? Do you...

Assad's G.S. Bashar al-Assad is... Yes. I'm a hand of God.

Ichikawa Do you believe in Allah?

10 「私はアッラーの一部」と主張するアサド守護霊

市川　では、あなたが信じる神の名前を教えていただけませんか。あなたは、神、神、神、といわれますが、名前をおっしゃっていません。

アサド守護霊　ああ、神の名前は隠されている。そう、神の名前は、歴史的に隠されてきた。今、神の名前は、バッシャール・アル・アサドとして現れた。それが、神の別名だ。

市川　アッラーのことを言っているのでしょうか。あなたは……。

アサド守護霊　バッシャール・アル・アサドは……、そう、私は「神の手」なんだ。

市川　あなたは、アッラーを信じていらっしゃいますか。

Assad's G.S. I am one of God's hands. Yes.

Ichikawa I want to confirm: Do you believe in Allah?

Assad's G.S. Of course, I'm Allah. One of the Allah, so…

Ichikawa Oh, you are Allah Himself?

Assad's G.S. I, I, I'm a part of Allah. A president. Hmm. American president and Syrian president are quite different. American president is a talent-like president. They get popularity votes and they run to get the popularity of the nation. But the real God never suffers such humiliation. God is dignity itself.

Ishikawa I think Allah is a Universal God. And I think He is more broad-minded.

10 「私はアッラーの一部」と主張するアサド守護霊

アサド守護霊 私は「神の手」の一つなんだ。そうだ。

市川 確認させてください。あなたは、アッラーを信じていらっしゃいますか。

アサド守護霊 もちろん、私がアッラーだ。アッラーの一人だ。だから……。

市川 おお、あなたが、アッラーその方ですか。

アサド守護霊 私、私、私は、アッラーの一部だ。大統領だ。うーん、アメリカの大統領とシリアの大統領は、全然違うんだよ。アメリカの大統領は、タレント的な大統領だ。人気投票を受け、選挙に出て、国民の人気を得なければならないからね。だが、本物の神は、そんな辱めは決して受けない。神は威厳そのものである。

石川 アッラーは、普遍的な神で、もっと心が広いと思います。

Assad's G.S. Allah should perish Christian countries. At that time, He'll be almighty.

11 The Nobel Peace Prize Winner President Obama is a Bad Guy

Ishikawa OK. I have another question. According to CBS news last week, maybe? Yes, you were interviewed, right? You warned that you would retaliate. If America conducted air strikes or limited attacks, maybe you will retaliate. What kind of retaliation are you going to carry out? For example, attacking Israel or triggering World War III.

Assad's G.S. Hmm, America has no money. So, they should abandon Mr. Obama. He should throw away everything and convert to Buddhism. Buddhists can throw away everything. So, he should throw away all military weapons and become a religious person like Buddhists. That's his way, I think. So, he

アサド守護霊　アッラーは、キリスト教国を滅ぼすべきだね。そのとき、全能となるんだ。

11　ノーベル平和賞受賞のオバマ大統領は「悪いやつ」

石川　分かりました。もう一つ質問があります。CBSニュースによりますと、確か先週でしたか、あなたはインタビューを受けましたね。あなたは、「報復する」と警告していました。もし、アメリカが空爆あるいは限定的な攻撃を行った場合、あなたは報復するでしょう。どのような報復をするおつもりですか。たとえば、イスラエルを攻撃するとか、第三次世界大戦の引き金を引くとか。

アサド守護霊　うーん、アメリカには金がないから、オバマさんを見捨てないといけないな。彼はすべてを投げうって、仏教に改宗すべきだな。仏教徒は、すべてを投げうつことができるから、彼も軍事兵器をすべて投げうって、仏教徒のような宗教的な人間になればいいんだよ。それが、彼の道だと思うな。だから、我々とは関係ない。

has nothing to do with us. We have no relation to him. We have no friendship and no anti-friendship relation. He's just a foreigner, an alien-like person to us. Never come back here! Go back to America!

Ishikawa But maybe you don't have global justice, I think. I don't think you are Allah.

Assad's G.S. American fleets should go back to the United States.

Ishikawa Maybe another, stronger president will come after Barack Obama.

Assad's G.S. He's a bad, bad guy. He's a very bad guy. He received a Nobel Peace Prize, but in reality he is a bad guy. A person who received a Nobel Peace Prize wants to attack our country. It's bad. It's a bad thing.

11　ノーベル平和賞受賞のオバマ大統領は「悪いやつ」

我々はオバマとは無関係だ。友人関係にもないし敵対関係にもない。彼は、我々にとって外国人、異邦人（いほうじん）というだけだ。二度と戻（もど）ってくるな！　アメリカに帰れ！

石川　しかし、あなたは、おそらく地球的正義をお持ちではないと思います。あなたはアッラーではないと思います。

アサド守護霊　アメリカ艦隊（かんたい）は、アメリカに帰るべきだな。

石川　バラク・オバマの後、たぶんまた別のより力強い大統領が出てきます。

アサド守護霊　彼は悪い、悪い、非常に悪いやつだ。ノーベル平和賞を受賞してはいるが、実際は、悪いやつだ。ノーベル平和賞をもらったやつが、我が国を攻撃しようとしているんだ。それは悪い、悪いことだ。

Ishikawa But from the viewpoint of global justice, a lot of countries have joined the Chemical Weapons Convention. But your country isn't in it. Do you have the intention to join the CWC?

Assad's G.S. It's OK. It's our inner problem. It's our country's inner problem.

Ishikawa Russian President Putin will not allow the use of chemical weapons.

Assad's G.S. No, no, Russia used a lot of weapons, chemical weapons in these several decades against other...

Ishikawa But I don't think he will allow the use of chemical weapons.

Assad's G.S. Ah, Japan also used chemical weapons against China.

11　ノーベル平和賞受賞のオバマ大統領は「悪いやつ」

石川　しかし、地球的正義の観点から、多くの国が化学兵器禁止条約に加盟しています。しかし、あなたの国は参加していません。あなたは参加する気はありますか？

アサド守護霊　それは問題ない。我が国の内部の問題、国内問題だ。

石川　ロシアのプーチン大統領は、化学兵器の使用を許さないでしょう。

アサド守護霊　いやいや、ロシアは、ここ数十年で、兵器、化学兵器をたくさん使ってるよ。他の……。

石川　しかし、「彼は化学兵器の使用を許さない」と思います。

アサド守護霊　ああ、日本も中国に対して化学兵器を使ったよな。

Kobayashi Never. We never used it.

Ichikawa An experiment...

Assad's G.S. Huh?

Ichikawa Some people just claim that Japan conducted an experiment.

Assad's G.S. Experiment? Yeah, yeah. We just did an "experiment," too. We also did an experiment on anti-government people.

Kobayashi Either way, Japan did not conduct any human experiments.

Ichikawa Yes, you killed so many people, even civilian people.

Ishikawa We have never used chemical weapons.

小林　絶対に、絶対に使ってません。

市川　実験を…

アサド守護霊　うん？

市川　実験をしたと言っている人がいるだけです。

アサド守護霊　実験？　そう、そう、我々も"実験"しただけなんだよ。我々も、反政府の人間たちに実験をしたわけだ。

小林　いずれにせよ、日本は人体実験などしていませんよ。

市川　あなたは、多くの人たち、民間人までも殺しましたね。

石川　我々は、決して、化学兵器を使っていません。あ

You are referring to World War II right?

Assad's G.S. No one believes that.

Ishikawa Before World War II.

Assad's G.S. No one believes that. Ha!

Ishikawa It was just propaganda.

Assad's G.S. Ah, anyway, Russia still has power. So, Mr. Obama will be defeated. He will resign from presidency. Ha, ha, ha, ha. He made a mistake.

Ishikawa I have another question. Who is guiding you spiritually?

Assad's G.S. Spiritually guiding me?

Ishikawa Yes. Do you receive some guidance?

なたは、第二次世界大戦前のことを言いたいのですね。

アサド大統領　そんなこと、信じるやつはいないよ。

石川　第二次世界大戦前のことを。

アサド大統領　そんなこと、誰も信じやしないぞ。ハッ！

石川　それはプロパガンダにすぎません。

アサド守護霊　ああ、とにかく、ロシアには、まだ力がある。だから、オバマさんは負けて、大統領を辞めるだろう。ハッハッハッハッ。彼はミスを犯したね。

石川　もう一つ質問があります。誰があなたを霊的に指導しているのでしょうか。

アサド　霊的に私を指導？

石川　はい。あなたは、何らかの指導を受けておられる

Assad's G.S. My father? My father? My father.

Ishikawa You receive guidance from your father?

Assad's G.S. My father, my brother and the ancient kings.

Ishikawa So do you believe in reincarnation?

Assad's G.S. In the Egyptian context, reincarnation is correct. Yeah, it's possible, possible, possible. Hmm… I might be the reincarnation of Tutankhamen.

(audience laughs)

Ishikawa So…

のでしょうか。

アサド守護霊　父親？　父親？　父親かな。

石川　自分の父親から指導を受けているのですか。

アサド守護霊　父親、兄弟、古代の王たちだ。

石川　では、あなたは転生輪廻(てんしょうりんね)を信じていますか？

アサド守護霊　エジプト的には、転生輪廻は正しい。そう、それはありうる、ありうる、ありうる。うーん、私は「ツタンカーメンの生まれ変わり」かもしれないなあ。

(会場笑)

石川　そうすると……。

Assad's G.S. (pointing towards the audience) Why do you laugh?

Ishikawa But basically, Muslim people do not believe in reincarnation.

Assad's G.S. Ah, oh…

Kobayashi The Alawites acknowledge it.

Assad's G.S. In some meaning, it's true.

Ichikawa I have heard that the Alawites believe in reincarnation.

Assad's G.S. Oh, oh, oh, oh, it's a difficult question. Our sect places importance on blood, blood, the blood-line from the ancient times. So, it's like the Japanese emperor system. So…

アサド守護霊 （会場を指して）なぜ笑う？

石川　しかし、イスラム教徒は、基本的には転生輪廻を信じません。

アサド守護霊　あー、えーっと……。

小林　アラウィ派の信者は、認めていた。

アサド守護霊　そう、それはある意味で本当だ。

市川　「アラウィ派の信者は転生輪廻を信じている」と聞きました。

アサド守護霊　えーっと、えーっと、えーっと、えーっと、それは難しい質問だな。まあ、我々の宗派は、古代からの血、血、血筋に重きを置くんだ。日本の天皇制みたいに。だから…。

Ishikawa Then, are you greater than Muhammad, the founder of Islam?

Assad's G.S. Muhammad, Muhammad… If I can defeat the American president, I am equal to Muhammad. Yes.

12 The Guardian Spirit of Assad Insists, "Syria Used to Be the 'Spiritual Center of the World,' Human Rights Are Something Unbelievable"

Ishikawa So what do you think of the future of Syria?

Assad's G.S. Glorious! God's power on our entire land. I will be the king of Arabic countries!

Ishikawa But without Putin's support, maybe you can't maintain your position, right? It's a very weak

石川　では、あなたは、イスラム教の開祖であるムハンマドよりも偉大なのですか。

アサド守護霊　ムハンマド、ムハンマドね……。私がアメリカの大統領を負かすことができたらムハンマドと同等だな。そうだ。

12　シリアはかつての「世界の霊的中心」、人権は「信じ難いもの」と主張するアサド守護霊

石川　では、シリアの将来はどうなると思われますか。

アサド守護霊　栄光だ！　神の力が、我が国をあまねく照らす。私はアラブ諸国の王となる！

石川　しかし、プーチンのサポートなくして、あなたはその立場を維持できないのではないですか。非常に弱い

gov…

Assad's G.S. Putin will become our servant, my servant, in the near future.

Ishikawa (wryly laughs) I think the opposite will be true. You will be the servant of Putin, right?

Assad's G.S. I'm a king and he's just a president.

Ishikawa The king of Syria, a small country, right?

Assad's G.S. But, historically, Syria is the center of the world! Damascus was the center of the religions of the world, and center of the spiritual power of the world, including Christianity, Japanese Shintoism, Buddhism, Hinduism, and all the religions.

Ishikawa But you will persecute other religions, right?

政……。

アサド守護霊　プーチンは、近い将来、我々の、私の、召し使いになるよ。

石川　（苦笑）逆だと思います。あなたがプーチンの召し使いですよね。

アサド守護霊　私は"王"だ。彼はただの大統領だろう。

石川　小さな国、シリアの王ですよね。

アサド守護霊　だが、歴史的には、シリアは世界の中心なんだよ！　ダマスカスは世界の宗教の中心だったし、世界の霊的パワーの中心だったんだ。キリスト教、日本神道、仏教、ヒンズー教などすべての宗教も含めて。

石川　しかし、あなたは他の宗教を迫害しますよね。

Assad's G.S. Persecute?

Ishikawa Yes, yes, of course, Sunni or…

Assad's G.S. For just a short period. To gain stability.

Ichikawa Then, I want to ask about human rights.

Assad's G.S. Human rights?

Ichikawa Yes, human rights. They are the freedom of…

Assad's G.S. What's that? It's oh…

Ichikawa Freedom of speech, you learned in the U.K.

Assad's G.S. I learned about it when I went to

アサド守護霊　迫害？

石川　そうそう、もちろんスンニ派や……。

アサド守護霊　安定を得るために、少しの間はね。

市川　では、「人権」について質問させてください。

アサド守護霊　人権？

市川　そうです。人権です。それは、自由……。

アサド守護霊　何のことだ？　それは、えーと……。

市川　「言論の自由」を、あなたはイギリスで学ばれました。

アサド守護霊　ロンドンに行ったときに学んだぞ。「人……。」

12 The Guardian Spirit of Assad Insists, "Syria Used to Be the 'Spiritual Center of the World,' Human Rights Are Something Unbelievable"

London. Human...

Ichikawa Rights.

Assad's G.S. Human rights, yes (laughs) but it's very, how do I say, stupid, absurd... I cannot choose the correct words but it's something unbelievable because the U.K. is a young country with a very short history; only 1,000 years of history. We have more than 3,000 years of history, so the modern system or political system of that kind of young country which was made in these 200 or 300 years is not effective all the time.

American President Obama said that the United States is the oldest democratic country, but it's wrong. The oldest democratic country is Greece. He has nothing in his brain. He is not a learned person. We are more ancient in history than the democratic country of Greece. We are the spiritual center of the world.

12 シリアはかつての「世界の霊的中心」、人権は「信じ難いもの」と主張するアサド守護霊

市川　「権」。

アサド守護霊　「人権」。そうか(笑)そんなものは、何というか、くだらん、馬鹿げた……、うまい言葉が見つからないけど、要するに信じ難いものだよ。イギリスなんてのは若い国で、ほんの短い歴史、たった1000年の歴史しかない。我々には3000年以上の歴史があるわけで、そんな若い国の、ここ2、300年の間に作られた近代的な制度や政治制度が、常に効果があるとは限らんのだ。

　アメリカのオバマ大統領は、「アメリカがいちばん古い民主主義国だ」と言っているが、それは間違ってる。いちばん古い民主主義国家はギリシャだよ。彼の頭は空っぽだな。博学な人間じゃないね。我々は、民主主義国家・ギリシャよりも歴史の古い、世界の霊的中心なんだよ。

Ishikawa Yes, it might have been so a long, long time ago, but now I think it's different. Tokyo is the new spiritual center of the world.

Assad's G.S. Ah, hmm… St. Paul came to Damascus and that was the starting point of Christianity. So, all the Christian people should have the heart of worship for Damascus, Syria.

Ishikawa Then do you accept the teachings of Christianity?

Assad's G.S. Ah, if they belong to me, it's OK.

Ichikawa I want to ask about your relationship with North Korea.

Assad's G.S. North Korea? It's far away, so…

石川　はい、遠い遠い昔はそうだったかもしれませんが、今は違うと思います。東京が、世界の新しい霊的中心地です。

アサド守護霊　ああ、うーん……。聖パウロがダマスカスに来たのが、キリスト教の始まりになったんだ。だから、キリスト教徒は、みんな、シリアのダマスカスを崇拝する心を持たなけりゃいかんな。

石川　では、あなたは、キリスト教の教えを受け入れるのですか？

アサド守護霊　ああ、「私のものになる」というなら、構わんよ。

市川　北朝鮮との関係についてお伺いしたいのですが。

アサド守護霊　北朝鮮？　遠いなあ。だから……。

Ichikawa It's far away, but you just imported missiles from them. Is there some other contract? Are there some other contracts between North Korea and Syria, such as inviting military advisors?

Assad's G.S. A little bit. A little. A bit.

Ichikawa If possible, could you tell us more?

Assad's G.S. Ah, there is a relationship between Syria, ah, no, Iran and North Korea. And we gain some things from Iran.

Ichikawa So you have an indirect connection with North Korea. There is a connection between Syria and Iran, and Iran and North Korea.

Assad's G.S. Indirect connection. Yes.

Ichikawa How about China?

市川　遠いですが、あなたはミサイルを輸入したばかりです。他にも契約はあるのですか。北朝鮮とシリアの間に、他の契約はあるのでしょうか。軍事顧問を招聘するとか。

アサド守護霊　少し、少し、少しはね。

市川　もう少し教えていただけませんか。

アサド守護霊　ああ、シリアと、じゃなかった、イランと北朝鮮は関係があるな。それでイランからシリアに、流れてくるものはあるよ。

市川　それでは、あなたは、「北朝鮮との間に間接的関係がある」ということですね。「シリアとイラン」の関係、「イランと北朝鮮」の関係というように。

アサド守護霊　間接的な関係。そうだな。

市川　中国とはどうでしょうか。

Assad's G.S. China?

Ichikawa Yes. Are you receiving some kind of investment or support, or are you in an agreement?

Assad's G.S. China has ambition, and they want to have sovereignty over the E.U. So, they are aiming to intrude into the Mediterranean Sea and intrude into the countries surrounding the Mediterranean Sea. For example, Turkey, Syria, Greece, Italy and Spain. That is China's plan, so I'm using their power. I want to use their power after Russia cooperates with us because they would assist us at the U.N. Permanent members like Russia and China are friends with us, so I can trust them.

13 Japan Should Fight Against America Again and Kill Obama

Ishikawa I want to ask about the relationship with

アサド守護霊　中国？

市川　はい。何らかの投資や援助を受けていたり、契約を結んでいたりしませんか。

アサド守護霊　中国には野心があって、EUを支配したがっている。それで、地中海や、地中海を取り巻く国々に侵入しようと狙っているわけだ。たとえば、トルコやシリア、ギリシャ、イタリア、スペインなどの国。それが中国の計画だから、私は中国の力を利用しているわけよ。ロシアの協力の次は、中国の力も利用したいね。中国は、国連で我々に協力してくれるからな。常任理事国のロシアと中国は、我々の友人だから、信用できるわな。

13　日本に望むことは「アメリカともう一度戦ってオバマを殺せ」

石川　日本との関係についてお伺いしたいと思います。

Japan. Historically the relationship between Japan and Syria has been very good. Yes. There have not been so many problems. So what do you think of the relationship with Japan? What do you expect?

Assad's G.S. It's a great country. A great, great Asian country. The country of yellow-colored people is very great. Please fight against America again! Please fight a second match with the United States.

Ishikawa No, we have the Japan-U.S. Security Treaty. So we will not fight against the U.S.

Assad's G.S. Please abandon that treaty.

Ishikawa No, no, we will not abandon it.

Assad's G.S. Please kill Obama.

Ishikawa We need to contain China. So, yes, this

13 日本に望むことは「アメリカともう一度戦ってオバマを殺せ」

日本とシリアの関係は、歴史的に見て非常に良好です。さほど問題もありません。そこで、日本との関係をどのようにお考えでしょうか。何を期待していますか？

アサド守護霊　偉大な国だよ。偉大な、偉大なアジアの国だ。この黄色人種の国は非常に偉大だ。ぜひ、アメリカともう一度戦ってほしい！　アメリカと、ぜひ、第二戦をやってほしいなあ。

石川　いえ、日米安保条約がありますので。だから、アメリカとは戦いません。

アサド守護霊　そんな条約なんか捨ててしまいなさいよ。

石川　いえ、いえ、捨てません。

アサド守護霊　ぜひ、オバマを殺してくれ。

石川　私たちは、中国を封じ込める必要があります。で

relation…

Assad's G.S. Contain China! That's difficult. They are a very huge country. It's impossible to contain them. You are very small.

Ishikawa No, no, no. We will contain China by the Japan-U.S. Security Treaty and by forming alliances with other Western countries.

Assad's G.S. Oh, you are the Israel of Asia. Very small, but have strong powers…

Ishikawa Japan alone cannot contain China, but if we work together, I think it's possible.

Assad's G.S. Ah, impossible, impossible, impossible, impossible, impossible. If Russia and China have power…

すから、この関係は……。

アサド守護霊　中国封じ込めだと！　そいつは難しいな。彼らはものすごく巨大な国だろう。それは不可能だよ。あなたたちはすごく小さいから。

石川　いえいえいえ。私たちは、日米同盟や、他の西洋諸国との同盟によって中国を封じ込めます。

アサド守護霊　おお、あなたたちは「アジアのイスラエル」なのか。すごく小さいけれど、力は強い……。

石川　日本だけでは中国を封じ込められませんが、力を合わせて取り組めば、可能だと思います。

アサド守護霊　あー、無理、無理、無理、無理、無理。ロシアと中国に力があれば…。

Ishikawa But the relationship between Prime Minister Abe and President Putin is very good. I don't think Russia will support China.

Assad's G.S. Putin is our only friend now. So, it's very difficult, but if Putin can persuade Japan and if Japan can persuade the United States, then we will be safe at that time.

Ishikawa It's impossible for him to persuade Japan.

Assad's G.S. Mr. Abe should make decisions. He can say almost nothing. He can only understand the situation of America. Is this the (laughs) prime minister of Japan? Can he only say that? He can think of nothing, almost nothing (laughs)!

Ishikawa Yes. Instead of him, Master Ryuho Okawa said in his lecture in July this year, that you should step down.

13　日本に望むことは「アメリカともう一度戦ってオバマを殺せ」

石川　しかし、安倍首相とプーチン大統領は、非常に良い関係です。ロシアは中国を支持しないと思います。

アサド守護霊　プーチンは、今、我々の唯一の友人なんでね。だから、非常に難しいことではあるが、もし、プーチンが日本を説得できて、日本がアメリカを説得できたら、その時は、我々も安全だな。

石川　彼が日本を説得するのは無理です。

アサド守護霊　安倍さんは決断すべきだよ。彼はほとんど何も言えないじゃないか。ただアメリカの状況を理解しているだけだ。これでも（笑）日本国の首相かい？　あんなことしか言えないのかね？　彼は何も考えられないのか。ほとんど何も！（笑）

石川　ええ。彼の代わりに、大川隆法総裁先生が今年7月の御法話の中で、あなたに、「退陣すべきだ」とおっしゃいました。

Assad's G.S. Step down?

Ishikawa Yes, step down from your presidency. You should step down.

Assad's G.S. Step down! Why?

Ishikawa Because you killed more than 100,000 of your own people. You should feel guilty of your sin.

Assad's G.S. That's the right, the right as king.

Ishikawa Right as king… yes, Master is the King of kings so…

Assad's G.S. Oh, master, master…

Ishikawa So you should step down. And after that…

アサド大統領　退陣だって？

石川　ええ。「大統領を辞職すべきだ」と。あなたは退くべきです。

アサド守護霊　退陣だと！　なんで？

石川　自国民を 10 万人以上も殺したからです。あなたは、罪の意識を感じるべきです。

アサド守護霊　それは権利だ、王の権利なんだよ。

石川　王の権利……、ええ、マスター（大川総裁）は王の中の王ですから……。

アサド守護霊　おー、マスター、マスター……。

石川　ですから、あなたは退陣すべきです。そしてその後……。

Assad's G.S. Please go to the coffee shop and be the master of the coffee shop.

Ishikawa No, no, no, not master in that sense. The God of gods, King of kings in the heavenly world.

Assad's G.S. Oh, I didn't know about that. You, International Division, have never come to our country, and you haven't taught good teachings for us.

Ichikawa But in the Middle East area, there are already many members.

Assad's G.S. Many members? You mean five or ten?

Ichikawa More.

Assad's G.S. Your "many" means five or ten?

13 日本に望むことは「アメリカともう一度戦ってオバマを殺せ」

アサド守護霊　コーヒーショップに行って、コーヒーショップのマスターでもやっててください。

石川　いえいえ、そのマスターではありません。神の中の神、天上界における王の中の王です。

アサド守護霊　ほう、それは知らなかったねえ。あなたたち国際局は我々の国に来たことがないし、良い教えを説いてくれたこともないけどなあ。

市川　しかし、中東域においては、すでに信者がたくさんいます。

アサド守護霊　信者がたくさん？　じゃあ、5人とか10人とか？

市川　もっとです。

アサド守護霊　あなたの言うたくさんとは、5人とか10

Ichikawa No, I can't say exactly, but so many people believe in El Cantare, so soon you will also come to know the existence of El Cantare.

Assad's G.S. One, two, three, four, five, six, seven, eight, nine, ten? Many people believe in El Cantare. Oh! I see! I see, I see, I see. In Japanese context, this is "many." OK, OK. But in Syria, I'm the president, and I have more than ten million followers. So, I'm greater than Master.

Ichikawa In the United States, *The Washington Post* said that you are the twelfth worst dictator of the world.

Assad's G.S. Oh….

13 日本に望むことは「アメリカともう一度戦ってオバマを殺せ」

人のことかな？

市川 違います。正確な数は言えませんが、本当にたくさんの人々がエル・カンターレを信じていますから、あなたもすぐにエル・カンターレの存在を知ることになるでしょう。

アサド守護霊 1、2、3、4、5、6、7、8、9、10？ たくさんの人々がエル・カンターレを信じてる。ああ、なるほど！ 分かった、分かった、分かった。日本的に言えば、「たくさん」なんだろうね。分かった。分かった。しかし、シリアでは私が大統領で、私の信者は1000万人以上いる。だから、私のほうがマスターより偉大なわけだ。

市川 アメリカのワシントン・ポストには、あなたは「世界で12番目に悪い独裁者である」と書かれています。

アサド守護霊 ああ……。

Ichikawa What do you think of that?

Assad's G.S. *The Washington Post*? There's influence from Korea in *The Washington Post*.* South Korea is giving influence to *The Washington Post*. I know, I know. You should investigate!

Ichikawa OK. Master said, "If people are escaping from a country, then that country is a bad country."

Assad's G.S. Oh, no, no. Then please explain the Exodus led by Moses (laughs).

Ichikawa They built a new country. But, these refugees are just refugees. And there's no place for them to live.

Assad's G.S. OK, OK, the anti-government group can escape from our country, become like the Israeli

---

* It is generally said that *The Washington Times* is under the influence of Korea.

13 日本に望むことは「アメリカともう一度戦ってオバマを殺せ」

市川　それについてはどう思われますか？

アサド守護霊　ワシントン・ポストだって？　そのワシントン・ポストというのは、朝鮮の影響を受けているぞ。[注] 韓国がワシントン・ポストに影響を与えている。知ってる、知ってるぞ。調査しないといかん！

市川　分かりました。マスターは、「国民が逃げ出しているような国は、悪い国である」とおっしゃっています。

アサド守護霊　おお、いや、いや、それならモーセの「出エジプト」を説明してくれたまえ（笑）。

市川　彼らは新しい国を建設しました。しかし、こっちの避難民はただの避難民でしかないですし、住む場所もありません。

アサド守護霊　分かった、分かった。反政府団体は我々の国から逃げ出して、イスラエルの民のようになって、

[注]　朝鮮の影響を受けているのは、一般的には、ワシントン・タイムズ紙であると言われている。

people and build a new country in another country. That's OK. America will forgive them.

Ichikawa Then in the end, there will remain nobody except you in Syria.

Assad's G.S. No, no, no, no, no, no, no, no. 90% of the people support me.

Ichikawa So, do you have any intention to resign?

Assad's G.S. If America air strikes us, the people of this country will rally and would want to protect President Assad! "We must protect him from America! We must save our king!" They will say so.

14 Justice is to Kill Those Who Disobey the Orders of God

Assad's G.S. Is there any difference between our

別の国の中に新しい国を作り直したらいいさ。それは構わん。アメリカも彼らを許すだろうよ。

市川　それでは、最終的に、あなた以外、誰もシリアに残らないでしょう。

アサド守護霊　いや、いや、いや、いや、いや、いや、いや、いや、いや、国民の90％は私を支持してるんだから。

市川　それで、辞職する気はありますか？

アサド守護霊　もし、アメリカが我々を空爆すれば、わが国民は結集し、アサド大統領を守ろうとするであろう！「アメリカから守らなければならない！　我らの王を救わねばならない！」そう言うだろうね。

14　正義とは「神の命令に背く者を殺すこと」

アサド守護霊　我々とあなたたちの間で、何か意見に相

14 Justice is to Kill Those Who Disobey the Orders of God

opinions?

Ichikawa Then, I want to confirm your idea on justice. What is your justice? Do you have the right to kill the people of your country?

Assad's G.S. Justice. Obedience to the king, obedience to kings and obedience to God. This is justice.

Ichikawa But, that doesn't mean that you have the right to kill people. So...

Assad's G.S. We have the power to kill people.

Ichikawa Oh, you have the power to kill people?

Assad's G.S. Oh, of course.

Ichikawa Who granted you such a power?

違はあるのかな？

市川　では、あなたの正義に対する考えを確認したいと思います。あなたの正義とは何ですか？　あなたには、自国民を殺す権利があるのですか？

アサド守護霊　正義ね。王への服従、王たちへの服従、神への服従。これが正義です。

市川　しかし、だからと言って、あなたに、「国民を殺す権利がある」ということにはなりません。ですから……。

アサド守護霊　我々には国民を殺す力があるのだ。

市川　あなたには、人々を殺す力があるのですか？

アサド守護霊　おお、当たり前だ。

市川　誰がそのような力を与えたのですか？

Assad's G.S. In the Middle East, bad people should be killed by the order of God.

Ichikawa Then which God ordered you?

Assad's G.S. Every god!

Ichikawa Every god!

Assad's G.S. Every god of every country can kill people who disobey gods' orders. Even the princess must be killed.

Ishikawa I think that's Satan, not a god.

Assad's G.S. Oh really?

Ishikawa Yes. God will not order you to kill people.

Assad's G.S. That's a misunderstanding of

14　正義とは「神の命令に背く者を殺すこと」

アサド守護霊　中東では、悪いやつらは神の命によって殺されるべきなんだよ。

市川　それでは、どの神があなたに命令しましたか？

アサド守護霊　あらゆる神だ！

市川　あらゆる神！

アサド守護霊　あらゆる国の、あらゆる神は、神々の命令に背く者たちを殺すことができる。王女でさえ、殺されねばならないのだ。

石川　それは、神ではなくサタンだと思います。

アサド守護霊　そうか？

石川　ええ。神は、「人を殺せ」と命じないでしょう。

アサド守護霊　それは民主主義に対する誤解だよ。あな

democracy. You've never learned about the hidden part of democracy. In another meaning, democracy is the cutting off of the head of God. This thought comes from Kant's philosophy. Hmm. Look at the French Revolution. That is the reality of democracy. Massacre! Massacre of the kings! And the massacre of the relatives of the king!

Ishikawa I don't know much about the French Revolution, but in America, there are many people who believe in God. And, at the end of speeches, presidents say, "God bless America." So, they do not deny God, I think.

Assad's G.S. And they say, "Amen"? Amen, they say Amen. Amen. Amen comes from Amun-Ra of Egypt, the one God system of Egypt.

Ishikawa I don't think so.

たたちは、民主主義の隠された部分を学んだことがないんだろう。別の意味においては、民主主義とは神の首をはねることなんだから。この考えはカント哲学から来ている。うん。だからフランス革命を見てみなさいよ。あれが民主主義の現実なんだよ。虐殺！　王たちの虐殺！そして王の一族の虐殺！

石川　フランス革命についてはよく分かりませんが、アメリカにおいては神を信じる人が大勢います。そして、大統領は演説の終わりに、「アメリカに神の祝福あれ」と言います。ですから、彼らは神を否定していないと思います。

アサド守護霊　そして、アーメンと言うわけか？　アーメン、彼らはアーメンと言うだろう。アーメン、アーメンとはエジプトのアモン・ラー、エジプトの一神教に由来しているんだ。

石川　私は、そうは思いませんが。

Assad's G.S. It's Amun of Egypt.

Ishikawa Do you have proof?

Assad's G.S. Yes. It's a historical truth. Amen comes from Amun-Ra worship. Amun-Ra worship perished within ten years and this kind of thinking came down to Syria, Israel and around this area from Egypt. This is the starting point of the one God system.

Ishikawa Yes, we also believe in the Supreme God, and the Supreme God guides Egypt, India, Greece and other Western countries. But maybe, now, you do not receive guidance from the Supreme God.

Assad's G.S. You know King David? King David integrated Israel more than 3,000 years ago and his last residence was in Damascus, Syria. It's very difficult,

アサド守護霊 エジプトの「アモン」だ。

石川 証拠はあるのですか？

アサド守護霊 ある。それは歴史的真実だよ。アーメンはアモン・ラー信仰のアモンからきている。アモン・ラー信仰は10年くらいで滅ぼされてしまったが、その考え方がエジプトからシリアやイスラエルやその周辺に流れてきた。これが、一神教の始まりなんだから。

石川 ええ、私たちも至高神を信じておりますが、その至高神がエジプト、インド、ギリシャ、そして他の西洋国家を導いてこられました。しかし、おそらく、あなたは現在は至高神のご指導を受けていないのではないでしょうか。

アサド守護霊 ダビデ王を知っているかな？ ダビデ王は3000年以上前にイスラエルを統合して、晩年はシリアのダマスカスに住んでいたんだ。とても難しい話なんだ

but historically, it was said that King David died 3,000 years ago, but in reality, he died more than 3,600 years ago. At that time, when he died in Syria, he was reborn as Ramses I, and lived his life as Ramses I at that time. David became old, and he almost died. And before he died, his soul was transferred into Ramses I, and he reigned in Egypt. This is the historical truth of religion. So, now you think that the origin of Christianity and Judaism is from Egypt, but in reality, it came from Damascus to Egypt. This is the spiritual truth.

Ichikawa I want to ask you about the United Nations. So the United Nations cannot show you…

Assad's G.S. Very, very new countries with only the talent and thinking power of a three-year-old. They should follow us. We have more than 3,000 years of history. We are superior to them. They cannot judge us! They don't have enough history,

が、歴史的には、ダビデ王は3000年前に亡くなったと言われているが、実際は、3600年以上前に亡くなったというのが真相だ。その時、彼はシリアで亡くなると、ラムセス一世として生まれ変わり、ラムセス一世として生きたのだ。ダビデは年を取って、死にかけたんだが、死ぬ前に、彼の魂(たましい)はラムセス一世に姿を変えて、エジプトを統治したんだ。これは宗教の歴史的真実だ。今のあなたたちは、「キリスト教とユダヤ教は、エジプトに起源がある」と考えているけれども、実は、ダマスカスからエジプトに入っていたんだ。これが霊的真実であるわけだな。

市川 国連についてお伺いします。国連はあなたに……。

アサド守護霊 非常に新しい国々で、能力や考え方は、ほとんど3歳児と変わらんな。彼らは我々に従うべきだ。我々には3000年以上の歴史があるんだよ。我々のほうが彼らよりも優れているんだ。彼らに、我々を裁くことなどできようはずがない！　彼らは、歴史が十分ではない

enough God, enough religion!

Ichikawa The U.N. cannot show you effective solutions.

Assad's G.S. The U.N. is a very bad league of countries. The U.N. was bad and is bad. Because the U.N. is killing you Japanese people! They are a bad, bad, organization! Don't use money for them! Stop sending money to the U.N.! This money should be transferred to Syria!

15 The Guardian Spirit of Assad Persistently Denies Killing His Own People

Ishikawa Anyway, we want to prevent the killing of many innocent people, so...

Assad's G.S. Innocent?

のだ！　神も宗教も十分じゃない！

市川　国連は、あなたがたに効果的な解決策を示すことができていません。

アサド守護霊　国連は、国家の連合体としては、ひどいもんだよ。国連は、昔も今も悪い。だって、国連はあなたがた日本人を殺しているからね！　彼らは悪の組織だ！　彼らに金を出してはいけない！　国連への金は止めろ！　その金はシリアに送金するべきだ！

15　「私は自国民を殺していない」と執拗に否定するアサド守護霊

石川　とにかく、私たちは、多くの罪のない人々が虐殺されるのを防ぎたいのです。ですから……。

アサド守護霊　罪のない？

Ishikawa Yeah.

Assad's G.S. Why? How can you say they are innocent? Innocent? How can you say they are innocent?

Ishikawa Because they did not do anything bad.

Assad's G.S. (pointing to himself) King! (pointing to the floor) And common, ordinary people. How can you say they are innocent?

Ishikawa Many people do not admit or regard you as a king. Some people may admit that fact...

Assad's G.S. I'm the most, most, most, most clever, near-to-God, supreme being of humankind.

Ishikawa But the role of the king is to realize the

石川　はい。

アサド守護霊　なぜだ？　なぜ罪がないと言える？　罪がない？　なぜそんなことが言えるんだ？

石川　なぜなら、彼らは何も悪いことはしていません。

アサド守護霊　（自分を指して）王だぞ！（床の方を指して）そして、普通の庶民だ。なぜ、罪がないのだ？

石川　多くの人々は、あなたを王と見なしてなどいません。なかには、そう認めている人もいるかもしれませんが……。

アサド守護霊　私は人類のなかで、最高に最高に最高に賢くて、神近き、至高なる存在である。

石川　ただ、王の役割は人間の幸福の実現、多くの人々

happiness of humans, happiness of many people, right? Like King David or…

Assad's G.S. That's your opinion. A small opinion, a very small opinion. Egyptian gods brought upon a lot of disasters, you know? Moses did, too.

Ichikawa OK. Thank you very much. Lastly, do you have any messages towards the international society?

Assad's G.S. Death to Obama! That's all.

Ishikawa Anyway, stop killing your own people.

Assad's G.S. I never kill people. My soldiers killed them.

Ishikawa Stop using chemical weapons. So Mr. Obama, President Obama is weak but…

15 「私は自国民を殺していない」と執拗に否定するアサド守護霊

の幸福の実現ですよね？ そうですよね？ ダビデ王のような……。

アサド守護霊 それは、君の意見だろう。つまらん意見、実に、つまらん意見だねえ。エジプトの神々は多くの災害をもたらしただろう？ モーセもやったし。

市川 どうもありがとうございました。最後に、国際社会に対して、何か言いたいことはありますか？

アサド守護霊 オバマに死を！ 以上だ。

石川 とにかく、自国の人々を殺すのは、おやめください。

アサド守護霊 私は、決して、国民を殺したりなんかしてないよ。私の兵士たちが殺したんだ。

石川 化学兵器を使用するのをおやめください。オバマ大統領は弱いですが……。

Assad's G.S. Stop the United States from using air strikes. You are colleagues of the United States. Mr. Abe can stop America. "America, don't kill Syrian people." He can say so. "If you want to kill Syrian people, you should return your Nobel Peace Prize!"

Ishikawa Japanese people will not support you. Mr. Abe also says that he will not support you and that you should step down.

Assad's G.S. OK, OK, OK, OK. In the end, of course, I will go up to Heaven and become like the ancient kings. I will become one of the gods of this Middle East area. At that time, I will scold your Master, "You made a mistake in Japan!"

Ichikawa You will be scolded.

Assad's G.S. No, I will be scolding.

15 「私は自国民を殺していない」と執拗に否定するアサド守護霊

アサド守護霊 アメリカに空爆なんかさせるんじゃないよ。あなたたちはアメリカの仲間なんだから。安倍さんならアメリカを止められるよ。「アメリカよ、決してシリアの人々を殺してはならない」。彼ならそう言えるんだ。「シリア国民を殺したいなら、ノーベル平和賞を返すべきだ」ってね！

石川 日本国民はあなたを支持しないでしょう。安倍さんも、あなたを支持しない。あなたには「退陣すべきだ」と言っています。

アサド守護霊 分かった、分かった、分かった、分かった。最後は、もちろん、私は天国に昇って、古代の王みたいになるからさ。私は、この中東地域の神の１人になるわけだ。そうなったら、あなたたちの主を、「お前は日本で間違えたのだ！」と叱ってやるから。

市川 あなたのほうが叱られるでしょう。

アサド守護霊 いや、私が叱る。

Ichikawa You will be scolded.

Assad's G.S. (points at himself) Huh?

Ichikawa You will be scolded in the next life.

Assad's G.S. Really? I can't believe that. You have only five or ten followers.

Ichikawa There are more. I won't say exactly, but there are many.

Assad's G.S. No rights. No power.

Ishikawa So anyway, killing your own people will not be justified, so you will not go up to Heaven.

Assad's G.S. I never kill people! I never use chemical weapons. It's just the military people.

15 「私は自国民を殺していない」と執拗に否定するアサド守護霊

市川　あなたが叱られるんです。

アサド守護霊　（自分を指して）はあ？

市川　あなたが、来世、叱られるんです。

アサド守護霊　本当か？ そんなことは信じられないね。あなたたちには、信者がたったの5人か10人しかいないしさ。

市川　もっとです。正確な数は言いませんが、たくさんいます。

アサド守護霊　権利もない。力もない。

石川　とにかく、自国の人々を殺すことは正当化されません。ですから、あなたは天国には上がりません。

アサド守護霊　私は絶対、人々を殺してなんかいない！ 化学兵器なんて、絶対、使ってない。軍人がやっただけ

Ishikawa But you gave the order, right?

Assad's G.S. No, no, no. I just know about it, but I did nothing.

Ishikawa But according to Mr. Kerry's comment, Secretary of State...

Assad's G.S. Kerry is a very... (twirls finger by his head indicating craziness)

Ishikawa Three people, including you, are responsible for using chemical weapons. I think you must take responsibility for it.

Ichikawa OK. Thank you very much for today's interview.

だろうが。

石川　でも、あなたが命令したんでしょう？

アサド守護霊　違う、違う、違う。ただ知っているだけで、私は何もしてないよ。

石川　しかし、ケリー国務長官のコメントによると……。

アサド守護霊　ケリーは本当に……（頭がおかしいことを意味するポーズ）

石川　あなたを含めて３人が、化学兵器の使用に関して責任があります。あなたは、その責任を取らなくてはならないと思います。

市川　分かりました。本日はインタビューを受けていただき、ありがとうございました。

Assad's G.S. Why did I come here?

16 In His Past Life, He Was a Relative of Ramses of Egypt

Isis Thank you for your precious time. We learned much from your thoughts.

Assad's G.S. (speaking to Isis) I know you. I know you. I know you.

Isis OK. Thank you very much. OK.

Assad's G.S. From ancient times, I know you.

Isis I think it's time for you to go home, maybe.

Assad's G.S. Near the pyramids of Giza. I know you. I know you. I know you.

アサド守護霊　なんで私は、ここに来たわけ？

16　過去世は「エジプトのラムセスの一族だった」

イシス　貴重なお時間をありがとうございました。私たちは、あなたのお考えから多くのことを学びました。

アサド守護霊　（イシスに向かって）あなたのことは知ってる。知ってる。知ってるよ。

イシス　分かりました。ありがとうございました。分かりました。

アサド守護霊　古代のことだ。あなたを知っているぞ。

イシス　そろそろ、お帰りの時間だと思います、たぶん。

アサド守護霊　ギザのピラミッドの近くだった。あなたを知ってる。知ってる。知ってるぞ。

Ichikawa Then...

Kobayashi At that time, who were you?

Assad's G.S. Huh?

Kobayashi At that time, who were you? If you know her.

Ichikawa Ancient time.

Assad's G.S. I was a relative of Ramses.

Kobayashi Which Ramses?

Assad's G.S. I... between I and II.

Kobayashi Oh, really?

Assad's G.S. Really.

16　過去世は「エジプトのラムセスの一族だった」

市川　それでは……。

小林　その当時、あなたは、どなたでしたか？

アサド守護霊　ああ？

小林　その当時、あなたは、どなただったのですか？
もし、彼女を知っているのなら。

市川　古代に。

アサド守護霊　私はラムセスの一族だ。

小林　どのラムセスですか？

アサド守護霊　一世……、一世と二世の間、だった。

小林　え、本当ですか？

アサド守護霊　本当だよ。

Kobayashi Oh.

Assad's G.S. Really. I know her. I know her. She was a healer.

Kobayashi A relative... a relative of Ramses should be right, generous and full of mercy.

Assad's G.S. It's a god. It's a god. It's a god.

Kobayashi A merciful god. But you are not.

Assad's G.S. "Merciful" is... I don't like that word. It's being used too easily.

Kobayashi Anyway you once lived in the time between Ramses I and Ramses II.

Assad's G.S. Yes. Yes.

16 過去世は「エジプトのラムセスの一族だった」

小林　おお。

アサド守護霊　本当だ。彼女を知っている。彼女はヒーラー（治療者）だった。

小林　一族……、ラムセスの一族なら、正しく、寛容で、慈愛に満ちた人間であるべきですが。

アサド守護霊　神だ。神だ。神だ。

小林　慈悲深い神です。でも、あなたは違いますね。

アサド守護霊　「慈悲深い」とは……その言葉は好きじゃないなあ。安易に使われ過ぎだ。

小林　とにかく、あなたは、かつて、ラムセス一世と二世の間の時代に生きていたと。

アサド守護霊　そう、そう。

Kobayashi Ah, OK.

Assad's G.S. At that time. Yes. I know you (pointing at Isis). I know you.

Ichikawa You know her? She's a disciple of El Cantare so please believe in El Cantare.

Assad's G.S. Oh, really?

Ichikawa Please convert to Happy Science.

Assad's G.S. I know you (to Isis). I know Ramses II, also. Ramses II, too. So, I'm very close to you. Very close to you. Your religion must have sprung from us.

Kobayashi But anyway Ramses surely is angry with you.

小林　そうですか、分かりました。

アサド守護霊　あの時。そうだ。(イシスを指して) あなたを知っている。知っている。

市川　彼女をご存じなんですか？　彼女はエル・カンターレの弟子です。ですから、エル・カンターレを信じてください。

アサド守護霊　おお、本当か？

市川　ハッピー・サイエンスに改宗してください。

アサド守護霊　(イシスに向かって) 知っている。ラムセス二世も知っているぞ。ラムセス二世もだ。だから、私はあなたたちと非常に近い。非常に近い関係だ。あなたたちの宗教は、我々から生じたに違いない。

小林　でも、とにかく、ラムセスは、きっとあなたのことを怒っていますよ。

Assad's G.S. Really?

Kobayashi Yes. Your action. Your attitude. Your attitude towards your nation's people.

Assad's G.S. Ramses killed millions of people so I cannot understand why that's so. Justice is to kill bad people. So I cannot understand.

17 "Push Prime Minister Abe to Persuade the United States"

Kobayashi OK. Anyway, we confirmed this time that you used chemical weapons, that you ordered to use chemical weapons and that you acknowledged that you don't mind even if you've killed more than 100,000 people of your own nation. That's enough, thank you.

Assad's G.S. Yes. Our military used chemical

アサド守護霊　本当か？

小林　ええ。あなたの行動、態度。あなたの国民に対する態度。

アサド守護霊　ラムセスは何百万も人を殺したわけだから、そんなことは理解できない。正義とは「悪人たちを殺すこと」なんだよ。だから、理解できないな。

17　「アメリカを説得するよう安倍首相に圧力を」

小林　分かりました。とにかく、今回、私たちは、「あなたが化学兵器を使用したこと」、「化学兵器の使用を命令したこと」、「自国民を10万人以上殺しても気にしていないと認めたこと」を、確認しました。それで十分です。ありがとうございました。

アサド守護霊　ああ。我々の軍隊は化学兵器を使ったよ。

weapons. This is true.

Ichikawa And you ordered...

Assad's G.S. Yes. I... I...

Kobayashi You're the supreme commander. You're the supreme commander.

Assad's G.S. I did not order. I just asked them. I did not order. I just asked.

Kobayashi In your constitution, "ask" means "order," right?

Assad's G.S. I just... I just threatened them. I just wanted to threaten them. And to kill bad people is not a bad thing under Islamic law.

Kobayashi You are liable for using chemical

それは事実だが。

市川　そして、あなたの命令で……。

アサド守護霊　ああ。私は……、私は……。

小林　あなたは最高司令官です。最高司令官ですよ。

アサド守護霊　私は命令なんかしていない。ただ頼んだだけだ。命令じゃなくて、頼んだだけだ。

小林　あなたの国の憲法では、「頼む」とは「命令する」ということでしょう？

アサド守護霊　ただ……、ただ脅しただけだよ。脅したかっただけなんだ。それに、悪人どもを殺すことは、イスラム法においては悪いことじゃないんだからさ。

小林　あなたは、化学兵器の使用に関して責任がありま

weapons. That's right.

Assad's G.S. But please accuse Mr. Obama. He wants to kill thousands of people in the near future. This is bad.

Ishikawa Your judgment... is not correct.

Assad's G.S. It's invasion. Invasion. No approval from countries around the world. U.N. No approval.

Ichikawa But please stop killing people in your own country. Is that OK?

Assad's G.S. OK, OK. In the meantime, I can stop, but I will, again. Because I'm God.

Ishikawa I think you will go to Hell.

17 「アメリカを説得するよう安倍首相に圧力を」

す。そういうことです。

アサド守護霊　だが、オバマさんを責めてくれよ。彼は近い将来、人々を何千人も殺したいと思っている。それは良くない。

石川　あなたの判断は……、正しくありません。

アサド守護霊　侵略だぞ。侵略。世界各国の承認を得ていない。国連の承認無しだ。

市川　でも、どうか、自国の国民を殺すのはやめてください。それはよろしいですか？

アサド守護霊　分かった、分かった。その間は、やめることはできる。でも、また、やるだろうな。何しろ、私は神だからね。

石川　あなたは地獄に堕ちると思います。

Assad's G.S. Hmm? I can't hear.

Isis Thank you so much for today.

Assad's G.S. Please understand us and be kind to us. We are from the same origin so be kind to us. And please persuade the United States. Please push Prime Minister Abe.

Ichikawa We are very kind but we have to show world justice.

Assad's G.S. World justice? There is no such thing as world justice. There is no justice. Only the superpower can do anything it wants. That is justice.

Ichikawa Doesn't justice come from God?

Assad's G.S. In the near future, you will be invaded by China. At that time, even if you want to

17　「アメリカを説得するよう安倍首相に圧力を」

アサド守護霊　なんだって？　聞こえなかった。

イシス　今日は本当にありがとうございました。

アサド守護霊　ぜひ、我々を理解して、親切にしていただきたい。我々の起源は同じなんだから、親切をお願いしますよ。そして、ぜひともアメリカを説得してくれ。ぜひ、安倍首相に圧力をかけてくれ。

市川　私たちは大変やさしくもありますが、世界的正義を示さなくてはなりません。

アサド守護霊　世界的正義？　世界的正義なんてものはないね。正義なんてない。超大国だけが、なんでも、やりたいことがやれるんだ。それが正義だよ。

市川　正義は神から来るのではないのですか？

アサド守護霊　近い将来、あなたたちは中国に侵略されるだろうね。その時には、たとえ正義を言いたくても、

say justice, no one would be able to hear you.

Ichikawa No, we will protect Japan.

Assad's G.S. You will be swallowed by China.

Ichikawa No.

Assad's G.S. At that time, you would want to do the same thing as me. You will surely attack using something, but it's impossible to defeat China.

Ichikawa We are determined to protect our nation.

Assad's G.S. Same with me.

Ichikawa But we don't kill people of our own country.

Assad's G.S. You will surely use chemical weapons

聞ける人は誰もいないだろうさ。

市川　いいえ、私たちは日本を守ります。

アサド守護霊　あなたたちは中国にのみ込まれるよ。

市川　いいえ。

アサド守護霊　そうなったら、あなたたちだって、私と同じことをしたくなるよ。きっと彼らを何かで攻撃するに違いない。でも、中国を負かすのは無理だね。

市川　私たちは、自分の国を守る決意を固めています。

アサド守護霊　私も同じだよ。

市川　しかし、私たちは、自分の国の人々は殺しません。

アサド守護霊　そうなったら、あなたたちは化学兵器を

at that time because you don't have Atomic Bombs (laughs).

Isis OK. I believe it's time.

Assad's G.S. Ah, is that so?

Isis • Ichikawa Thank you very much for today.

Assad's G.S. OK. Bye.

Ryuho Okawa (claps twice) OK.

18 After Interviewing the Guardian Spirit of President Assad

Ryuho Okawa Hmm. He is a very "crime of conscience" type of person. This is very shocking (sighs).

Well, he is definitely a dictator if you call him so. Maybe being a president for over ten years makes one

使うに違いない。だって原爆(げんばく)は持ってないもんなあ。(笑)

イシス　分かりました。もう時間です。

アサド守護霊　あぁ、そうか？

イシス・市川　本日は、ありがとうございました。

アサド守護霊　はい、さようなら。

大川隆法　(二拍手(にはくしゅ)をして) はい。

18　アサド大統領の守護霊インタビューを終えて

大川隆法　うーん、すごい確信犯的な方でございますね。これはすごいですね (ため息をつく)。
　まあ、独裁者といえば独裁者であることは、確実ですね。10年以上やったら、独裁者になるのでしょうか。彼は西

a dictator. He studied democracy in the West, but after returning to his own country, maybe he found out through experience that only tyranny works in Arabic countries.

This is where the difficulty lies. I think that, without reforming the entire Islam religion, Syria cannot become democratic. I believe there is a connection here politically.

Islam is in fact compatible with Communism. Their thinking is quite similar to it. Islam values equality more than prosperity. When equality is at the center of politics, Communism is more compatible, of course. Communism matches up very well with the dictator and the elite few. There are connections, so the Cold War might be continuing.

Unfortunately, I don't think he will live too long. I think he will be removed. He is a little old-fashioned. I guess just being an optometrist was not enough to change his thinking through his studies, even after studying abroad in the U.K. He only took

洋で民主主義を学んだのでしょうが、自国に戻ったら、「アラブの国では、専制でないとうまくいかない」と、経験を通じて気付くのかもしれません。

　この部分は、難しいところではあります。同じようにいかないのは、たぶん、イスラム教まで改革しない限り、民主主義制度には移行はできないんだと思います。政治的に、それと関係があるのでしょう。

　イスラムは、意外に、政治的には共産主義制度と合うんですよ。考え方がよく似ているんです。繁栄を考えるよりは、平等のほうが強いんです。だから、平等を中心にすると、やはり共産主義体制のほうが合うわけです。共産主義体制というのは、一部エリートと独裁者が非常に似合うので、このへんとは関係があるんでしょう。これは、冷戦の続きかもしれませんね。

　残念ですが、私の判断としては、それほど長くは生きられないのではないかと思います。取り除かれるだろうとは思います。ちょっと、頭が古いですね。やはり古いような気がします。イギリス留学をしても、眼医者さんだけでは、ちょっと無理だったのでしょうか、勉強は。「悪

back with him the thought of removing what is bad, although there might be such parts in politics, too.

In addition to that, compared to the Western society, people in the Islamic society very easily kill those who commit crimes. People very easily kill others in the Islamic society. Not just Syria, but other countries as well. They immediately come to kill you if you disobey God's teachings or break the law. This is a civil rights issue now that must be solved but it will not be so easy because both religion and politics need to be reformed. There is cultural tradition, too, so it's difficult.

I'm guessing that, in conclusion, Assad will be removed. So Mr. Putin should let go of this matter at an appropriate time. I know it might be hard for him to let go of this matter because Russia has a military port in Syria, but sadly, I think he should retreat.

President Assad's thinking was that of a dictator.

いところを取り除く」というような考えだけを持って帰ったようなところですので、まあ、それは、そういうところもあるのかもしれません。

　それと、やはり、「罪に対して殺してもいい」というところが問題です。西洋社会に比べてイスラム教社会では、非常に簡単に人を殺すのです。これは、シリアだけでなくて、ほかのところも、みんなそうです。神の教えや法律等に背いたら、すぐに殺しにくるのです。このへんのところは、今、人権の問題だろうと思いますが、それほど簡単にはいかない部分があると思います。宗教と政治と、両方からの改革がないといけません。それと、文化的伝統と、両方があるので、難しいでしょうね。

　ただ、結論的には、「取り除かれるであろう」と推定しますね。だから、プーチンさんは、適当なところで諦めなければいけないのではないでしょうか。軍港を持っているので、手放したくないのは分かるのですが、残念ながら、これは、やはり退くべきでしょうね。私はそう思います。

　まあ、「考え方は、いわゆる独裁者の考えであった」と

The Western society's voice on not forgiving him will get bigger after hearing this spiritual message. They would think, "He is almost the same as the bad old Saddam Hussein."

Everyone hesitates to take action because there is no evidence that Syria used chemical weapons, but (the guardian spirit of) President Assad clearly admitted to using them. There was no reluctance on this point. As for the question of whether or not he gave direct orders to kill people, he made an excuse saying, "It was the military that killed them, not me." I think it's just that he does not want to be hanged in case he gets caught.

It's very sad. At any rate, my verdict is that this regime will come to an end.

I know Mr. Obama might not want to take action since he won the Nobel Peace Prize, but if he overlooks these kinds of things, terrorist nations and similar autocratic states, one after another, will start misbehaving again. So he should stand firm. We must

18 アサド大統領の守護霊インタビューを終えて

いうことで、これを聞けば、おそらく、西洋社会では「前のサダム・フセインとほとんど同じだ」と思われて、許さない声が高まることでしょう。

「化学兵器を使ったかどうか、証拠がないから」と、みんなヘジテイト(躊躇(ちゅうちょ))していますが、アサド守護霊は「使った」ということをはっきりと認めましたのでね。ここに対しては、迷いはありませんでした。直接、命令したかどうかのところは、「殺したのは軍部であって、私は殺したわけではない」という言い訳が、ちょっとだけあるようですが、「捕まったときに、吊(つ)るされたくない」というだけのことかもしれません。

まあ、残念ですね。でも、「この政体は終わりかな」というのが、私の判断です。

オバマさんは、ノーベル平和賞をもらったのに、攻撃はやりたくないのでしょうけれども、やはり、こういうのを見過ごすと、テロ国家、ないしは、そういう独裁国家がまた次々と悪さをし始めるので、ここは頑張(がんば)らないといけないのではないでしょうか。世界が「警察がなく

stop the world from becoming like a city without police that is filled with violence. If the United States cannot stop this, then there would be nothing that any country could do even if there were to be any accidental firing in North Korea, China or Iran.

My thought is that they should have intervened much earlier. I think that the fact that Mr. Obama allowed this issue to come this far unfortunately shows his political weakness. This is just an opinion, but I hope it can be used in some way.

18　アサド大統領の守護霊インタビューを終えて

なった暴力の町」のように変わっていくことは、やはり止めるべきではないかと思います。これを止められなかったら、もし北朝鮮や中国や、あるいはイランで暴発が起きても、もはや、どこも、何もすることがなくなるのではないかという気はします。

　私は「もっと早く介入しておくべきだった」と思います。ここまで時間がかかったというのは、残念ながら、政治的に弱かったのではないでしょうか。まあ、一つの意見ではありますけれども、何らかの参考になればと思います。

アサド大統領のスピリチュアル・メッセージ

2013年9月21日　初版第1刷

著　者　　大川　隆法

発行所　　幸福の科学出版株式会社

〒107-0052　東京都港区赤坂2丁目10番14号
TEL(03)5573-7700
http://www.irhpress.co.jp/

印刷・製本　　株式会社 堀内印刷所

落丁・乱丁本はおとりかえいたします
©Ryuho Okawa 2013. Printed in Japan. 検印省略
ISBN978-4-86395-397-0 C0031
Photo：SANA/AP/アフロ
Photo：ロイター／アフロ

大川隆法ベストセラーズ・希望の未来を切り拓く

未来の法
新たなる地球世紀へ

暗い世相に負けるな！ 悲観的な自己像に縛られるな！ 心に眠る無限のパワーに目覚めよ！ 人類の未来を拓く鍵は、一人ひとりの心のなかにある。

2,000円

救世の法
信仰と未来社会

信仰を持つことの功徳や、民族・宗教対立を終わらせる考え方など、人類への希望が示される。地球神の説くほんとうの「救い」とは──。

1,800円

国を守る宗教の力
この国に正論と正義を

3年前から国防と経済の危機を警告してきた国師が、迷走する日本を一喝！ 国難を打破し、日本を復活させる正論を訴える。
【幸福実現党刊】

1,500円

幸福の科学出版

大川隆法 ベストセラーズ・世界で活躍する宗教家の本音

大川隆法の守護霊霊言
ユートピア実現への挑戦

あの世の存在証明による霊性革命、正論と神仏の正義による政治革命。幸福の科学グループ創始者兼総裁の本心が、ついに明かされる。

1,400円

政治革命家・大川隆法
幸福実現党の父

未来が見える。嘘をつかない。タブーに挑戦する──。政治の問題を鋭く指摘し、具体的な打開策を唱える幸福実現党の魅力が分かる万人必読の書。

1,400円

素顔の大川隆法

素朴な疑問からドキッとするテーマまで、女性編集長3人の質問に気さくに答えた、101分公開ロングインタビュー。大注目の宗教家が、その本音を明かす。

1,300円

※表示価格は本体価格（税別）です。

大川隆法 霊言シリーズ・英語説法・霊言

Power to the Future
未来に力を

英語説法集　日本語訳付き

予断を許さない日本の国防危機。混迷を極める世界情勢の行方──。ワールド・ティーチャーが英語で語った、この国と世界の進むべき道とは。

1,400円

バラク・オバマの スピリチュアル・メッセージ
再選大統領は世界に平和をもたらすか

弱者救済と軍事費削減、富裕層への増税……。再選翌日のオバマ大統領守護霊インタビューを緊急刊行！日本の国防危機が明らかになる。
【幸福実現党刊】

英語霊言　日本語訳付き

1,400円

サッチャーの スピリチュアル・メッセージ
死後19時間での奇跡のインタビュー

フォークランド紛争、英国病、景気回復……。勇気を持って数々の難問を解決し、イギリスを繁栄に導いたサッチャー元首相が、日本にアドバイス！

英語霊言　日本語訳付き

1,300円

幸福の科学出版

大川隆法 霊言シリーズ・中東問題の真相に迫る

イラク戦争は正しかったか
サダム・フセインの死後を霊査する

全世界衝撃の公開霊言。「大量破壊兵器は存在した!」「9.11はフセインが計画し、ビン・ラディンが実行した!」——。驚愕の事実が明らかに。

1,400円

イスラム過激派に正義はあるのか
オサマ・ビン・ラディンの霊言に挑む

「アルジェリア人質事件」の背後には何があるのか——。死後も暗躍を続ける、オサマ・ビン・ラディンが語った「戦慄の事実」。

1,400円

ロシア・プーチン新大統領と帝国の未来
守護霊インタヴュー

中国が覇権主義を拡大させるなか、ロシアはどんな国家戦略をとるのか!? また、親日家プーチン氏の意外な過去世も明らかに。
【幸福実現党刊】

1,300円

※表示価格は本体価格(税別)です。

大川隆法霊言シリーズ・中東問題の真相に迫る

中東で何が起こっているのか
公開霊言
ムハンマド／アリー／サラディン

イスラム教の知られざる成り立ちや歴史、民主化運動に隠された「神の計画」。開祖、四代目カリフ、反十字軍の英雄が、イスラム教のめざすべき未来を語る。

1,600円

イラン大統領 vs. イスラエル首相
中東の核戦争は回避できるのか

世界が注視するイランとイスラエルの対立。それぞれのトップの守護霊が、緊迫する中東問題の核心を赤裸々に語る。
【幸福実現党刊】

1,400円

世界紛争の真実
ミカエル vs. ムハンマド

米国（キリスト教）を援護するミカエルと、イスラム教開祖ムハンマドの霊言が、両文明衝突の真相を明かす。宗教対立を乗り越えるための必読の書。

1,400円

幸福の科学出版

大川隆法 霊言シリーズ・中国・北朝鮮情勢を読む

北朝鮮の未来透視に挑戦する
エドガー・ケイシー リーディング

「第2次朝鮮戦争」勃発か!? 核保有国となった北朝鮮と、その挑発に乗った韓国が激突。地獄に堕ちた"建国の父"金日成の霊言も同時収録。

1,400円

中国と習近平に未来はあるか
反日デモの謎を解く

「反日デモ」も、「反原発・沖縄基地問題」も中国が仕組んだ日本占領への布石だった。緊迫する日中関係の未来を習近平氏守護霊に問う。
【幸福実現党刊】

1,400円

周恩来の予言
新中華帝国の隠れたる神

北朝鮮のミサイル問題の背後には、中国の思惑があった! 現代中国を霊界から指導する周恩来が語った、戦慄の世界覇権戦略とは!?

1,400円

※表示価格は本体価格(税別)です。

幸福の科学グループのご案内

宗教、教育、政治、出版などの活動を通じて、地球的ユートピアの実現を目指しています。

宗教法人　幸福の科学

1986年に立宗。1991年に宗教法人格を取得。信仰の対象は、地球系霊団の最高大霊、主エル・カンターレ。世界100カ国以上の国々に信者を持ち、全人類救済という尊い使命のもと、信者は、「愛」と「悟り」と「ユートピア建設」の教えの実践、伝道に励んでいます。

（2013年9月現在）

愛

幸福の科学の「愛」とは、与える愛です。これは、仏教の慈悲や布施の精神と同じことです。信者は、仏法真理をお伝えすることを通して、多くの方に幸福な人生を送っていただくための活動に励んでいます。

悟り

「悟り」とは、自らが仏の子であることを知るということです。教学や精神統一によって心を磨き、智慧を得て悩みを解決すると共に、天使・菩薩の境地を目指し、より多くの人を救える力を身につけていきます。

ユートピア建設

私たち人間は、地上に理想世界を建設するという尊い使命を持って生まれてきています。社会の悪を押しとどめ、善を推し進めるために、信者はさまざまな活動に積極的に参加しています。

海外支援・災害支援

国内外の世界で貧困や災害、心の病で苦しんでいる人々に対しては、現地メンバーや支援団体と連携して、物心両面にわたり、あらゆる手段で手を差し伸べています。

自殺を減らそうキャンペーン

年間約3万人の自殺者を減らすため、全国各地で街頭キャンペーンを展開しています。

公式サイト **www.withyou-hs.net**

ヘレンの会

ヘレン・ケラーを理想として活動する、ハンディキャップを持つ方とボランティアの会です。視聴覚障害者、肢体不自由な方々に仏法真理を学んでいただくための、さまざまなサポートをしています。

公式サイト **www.helen-hs.net**

INFORMATION

お近くの精舎・支部・拠点など、お問い合わせは、こちらまで！

幸福の科学サービスセンター
TEL. **03-5793-1727** (受付時間 火~金:10~20時/土・日:10~18時)
宗教法人 幸福の科学公式サイト **happy-science.jp**

教育

学校法人 幸福の科学学園

学校法人 幸福の科学学園は、幸福の科学の教育理念のもとにつくられた教育機関です。人間にとって最も大切な宗教教育の導入を通じて精神性を高めながら、ユートピア建設に貢献する人材輩出を目指しています。

幸福の科学学園

中学校・高等学校（那須本校）
2010年4月開校・栃木県那須郡（男女共学・全寮制）
TEL **0287-75-7777**
公式サイト **happy-science.ac.jp**

関西中学校・高等学校（関西校）
2013年4月開校・滋賀県大津市（男女共学・寮及び通学）
TEL **077-573-7774**
公式サイト **kansai.happy-science.ac.jp**

幸福の科学大学（仮称・設置認可申請予定）
2015年開学予定
TEL **03-6277-7248**（幸福の科学 大学準備室）
公式サイト **university.happy-science.jp**

仏法真理塾「サクセスNo.1」
小・中・高校生が、信仰教育を基礎にしながら、「勉強も『心の修行』」と考えて学んでいます。
TEL **03-5750-0747**（東京本校）

不登校児支援スクール「ネバー・マインド」
心の面からのアプローチを重視して、不登校の子供たちを支援しています。
また、障害児支援の**「ユー・アー・エンゼル！」**運動も行っています。
TEL **03-5750-1741**

エンゼルプランV
幼少時からの心の教育を大切にして、信仰をベースにした幼児教育を行っています。
TEL **03-5750-0757**

NPO活動支援

学校からのいじめ追放を目指し、さまざまな社会提言をしています。また、各地でのシンポジウムや学校への啓発ポスター掲示等に取り組むNPO「いじめから子供を守ろう！ネットワーク」を支援しています。

公式サイト **mamoro.org**
ブログ **mamoro.blog86.fc2.com**
相談窓口 TEL.**03-5719-2170**

政治

幸福実現党

内憂外患(ないゆうがいかん)の国難に立ち向かうべく、2009年5月に幸福実現党を立党しました。創立者である大川隆法党総裁の精神的指導のもと、宗教だけでは解決できない問題に取り組み、幸福を具体化するための力になっています。

党員の機関紙「幸福実現NEWS」

TEL 03-6441-0754
公式サイト hr-party.jp

出版メディア事業

幸福の科学出版

大川隆法総裁の仏法真理の書を中心に、ビジネス、自己啓発、小説など、さまざまなジャンルの書籍・雑誌を出版しています。他にも、映画事業、文学・学術発展のための振興事業、テレビ・ラジオ番組の提供など、幸福の科学文化を広げる事業を行っています。

TEL 03-5573-7700
公式サイト irhpress.co.jp

入会のご案内

あなたも、幸福の科学に集い、ほんとうの幸福を見つけてみませんか？

幸福の科学では、大川隆法総裁が説く仏法真理をもとに、「どうすれば幸福になれるのか、また、他の人を幸福にできるのか」を学び、実践しています。

入会

大川隆法総裁の教えを信じ、学ぼうとする方なら、どなたでも入会できます。入会された方には、『入会版「正心法語」』が授与されます。（入会の奉納は1,000円目安です）

ネットでも入会できます。詳しくは、下記URLへ。
happy-science.jp/joinus

三帰誓願（さんきせいがん）

仏弟子としてさらに信仰を深めたい方は、仏・法・僧の三宝への帰依を誓う「三帰誓願式」を受けることができます。三帰誓願者には、『仏説・正心法語』『祈願文①』『祈願文②』『エル・カンターレへの祈り』が授与されます。

植福の会（しょくふくのかい）

植福は、ユートピア建設のために、自分の富を差し出す尊い布施の行為です。布施の機会として、毎月1口1,000円からお申込みいただける、「植福の会」がございます。

「植福の会」に参加された方のうちご希望の方には、幸福の科学の小冊子（毎月1回）をお送りいたします。詳しくは、下記の電話番号までお問い合わせください。

月刊「幸福の科学」
ザ・伝道
ヤング・ブッダ
ヘルメス・エンゼルズ

INFORMATION

幸福の科学サービスセンター
TEL. **03-5793-1727**（受付時間 火〜金：10〜20時／土・日：10〜18時）
宗教法人 幸福の科学 公式サイト **happy-science.jp**